Gourds with Southwestern Motifs
Rainsticks, Masks, Vessels & More

BONNIE GIBSON

Photographs by Everett Gibson

LARK BOOKS

A Division of Sterling Publishing Co., Inc.
New York / London

Designed by Judy Morgan

The Library of Congress has cataloged the hardcover edition as follows:

Gibson, Bonnie.
  Gourds : Southwest gourd techniques & projects from simple to sophisticated
/ Bonnie Gibson.
       p. cm.
  Includes index.
  ISBN 978-1-4027-2522-7
1. Gourd craft—Southwestern States. I. Title.

TT873.5.G53 2006
745.5—dc22

                                        2006010149

10 9 8 7 6 5 4 3 2 1

Published by Lark Books, A Division of
Sterling Publishing Co., Inc.
387 Park Avenue South, New York, N.Y. 10016

First Paperback Edition 2009
© 2006 by Bonnie Gibson

First published in 2006 by Sterling Publishing, Co., Inc.
Previously published as Gourds: Southwest Gourd Techniques & Projects from Simple to Sophisticated

Distributed in Canada by Sterling Publishing,
c/o Canadian Manda Group, 165 Dufferin Street
Toronto, Ontario, Canada M6K 3H6

Distributed in the United Kingdom by GMC Distribution Services,
Castle Place, 166 High Street, Lewes, East Sussex, England BN7 1XU

Distributed in Australia by Capricorn Link (Australia) Pty Ltd.,
P.O. Box 704, Windsor, NSW 2756 Australia

If you have questions or comments about this book, please contact:
Lark Books
67 Broadway
Asheville, NC 28801
(828) 253-0467

Manufactured in China

ISBN 13: 978-1-4027-2522-7 (hardcover) 978-1-60059-548-6 (paperback)

For information about custom editions, special sales, premium and corporate purchases, please contact
Sterling Special Sales Department at 800-805-5489 or specialsales@sterlingpub.com.

CONTENTS

PART ONE

Preparing Nature's Canvas

1 Introduction to Gourds

"What is that thing?"

Without exception, every one of my friends and family members reacted by blurting this question when I brought home my first raw gourd years ago. I had gone to an arts and crafts festival, where I picked up and admired some beautiful "native pottery." The pieces were so unexpectedly lightweight that I almost dropped them in surprise. The helpful artist provided my first exposure to gourd art and kindly sold me a couple of raw gourds so I could try creating my own. I was hooked immediately.

Primitive humans were the first to recognize the usefulness of gourds; in a wide variety of cultures across the millennia, gourds served as storage containers and water vessels. In time, humans came to use gourds as musical instruments and religious objects, as well. Even with crude tools, some of

Gourd drum necklaces.

these early gourd adaptations progressed from simple utilitarian objects to works of art. Gourds continue to have an important place in native cultures reaching from the Americas to Africa and Asia.

Artists have lately rediscovered the gourd, recognizing the versatility and beauty of this three-dimensional canvas. In gourds, nature provides a medium of enormous range in size, shape, and appearance, and one of the most versatile with which to work. Cut them, carve them, paint them, inlay them with stone—the gourd's possibilities are endless. Embellish them with such natural materials as leather, fur, antler, stone, feathers, and botanicals, or man-made items such as beads, metallic findings, hardware parts, and treasured garage sale finds; all can become attractive decorative accents. Color gourds with dyes, paints, stains, waxes, or metallic leafing; add structure with clay and wood. Transform gourds into functional objects, manipulate them into sculptural elements, or turn them into pieces of art subtly camouflaged as pottery, wood, or stone.

The idea of beginning a gourd project may intimidate those unfamiliar with tools or who possess limited crafting experience. Don't think that you need a fully loaded workshop with all the latest gadgets in order to turn out a pleasing project. Keep in mind that gourds have been decorated and used for thousands of years, and early man certainly didn't have the benefit of power tools!

Gourd Characteristics

VARIETIES AND IDENTIFICATION

Gourds are cucurbits, members of the *Cucurbitaceae* family, which includes squashes, pumpkins, melons, and cucumbers. They grow in an amazing variety of standard shapes and unusual cross-pollinated hybrids. Luffa sponge gourds (*Luffa cylindrica*) and colorful ornamental gourds are also members of this family, but the artist will find that gourds of the *Lagenaria* or hard-shell variety are the most suitable for crafting.

Ornamental gourds bloom during the day with large, showy, yellow-gold flowers; sold at roadside stands and in grocery stores, they are often used for fall decorating. Their shapes and markings are enormously diverse, and their coloring is usually a mixture of greens, whites, and yellow-oranges. Small in size, ornamental gourds often feature interesting surface warts or ridges.

Desert Friends.
Jackrabbit and hummingbird.

A commercial field growing young gourd plants, which are just beginning to vine and produce flowers.
Photo courtesy of Welburn Gourd Farm.

After successful pollination, the female flower produces gourd fruit.
Photo courtesy of Welburn Gourd Farm.

Related families of cucurbits produce small, round varieties known as coyote gourds (at low elevations) or buffalo gourds (at higher elevations). These sometimes grow wild along highways and other noncultivated areas. They bloom early in the day with bright yellow flowers, and the resulting fruit is palatable to some species of wildlife.

Loofah gourd plants bloom in daytime with beautiful orangey-yellow blossoms that produce a long, zucchini-like fruit. The outer shell of the dried loofah is thin and brittle, and is usually peeled away to reveal a fibrous inner pulp. The loofah "vegetable sponge" has great value as a bath product and scrubbing sponge. Ornamental and wild-growing varieties of loofah gourd tend to be extremely thin-shelled and are not suitable for the projects in this book.

In the growing season, large white, night-blooming flowers distinguish the hard-shell gourds in the fields. Their vines are prolific, spreading over a large area; they grow laterally on the ground, but will climb readily, given the opportunity. Their shapes and sizes provide hard-shell gourds their names and descriptions. Common varieties that are suitable for projects in this book include the bottle, canteen, kettle, cannonball, bushel basket, basketball, snake, and dipper.

Gourds are fun and interesting to grow, and it can increase your enjoyment and reward to raise your own art material. I encourage you to research the abundant literature available for further information on gourd culture and seed suppliers; local agricultural extension offices have general information relating to gourd growing. A particularly valuable resource is the American

These young gourds are reaching maturity. Photo courtesy of Welburn Gourd Farm.

Gourd Society (www.americangourdsociety.org), a national organization promoting interest in activities relating to gourds: cultivation, crafting and fine artistic decoration, competitive exhibition, and historical research. Other countries, including Canada, Australia, and Japan, have similar national associations, and I highly recommend membership in your national group.

GOURD CHARACTERISTICS AND CRAFTING

A multitude of growing factors affect a gourd's suitability for crafting, including temperature, humidity, fertilization methods, and soil conditions. Gourds grown in colder climates with shorter growing seasons differ vastly from those grown in more temperate zones. Fertile soil and ample rainfall produce a higher quality gourd.

Surface mold is a natural accompaniment to the dehydration and curing of a raw gourd. Gourds grown in regions with high humidity—a condition favorable to mold—are often easy to clean, since the molding process aids in breaking down the gourd skin. The mold does no harm and doesn't affect the quality of the gourd in any way; in fact, artists often seek out gourds with the interesting markings and discolorations it creates on the surface. These mold marks add effect and provide inspiration for artistic design. Gourds grown in hot, dry climates lose their moisture more rapidly, inhibiting mold growth. These conditions produce gourds with tough skins, which are much more difficult to remove.

The mature gourds have been cut from the dead vines and have already begun to dry. They will soon be ready for crafting. Photo courtesy of Welburn Gourd Farm.

Pests may burrow or bore holes in growing gourds, and minor shriveling marks may occur as gourds dry. Inspect each gourd carefully beforehand to determine whether bug bites, scratches, or other flaws may detract from your finished project. You can salvage less than perfect gourds by filling small holes, carving away unwanted material, or painting over blemishes. In some cases, flaws can add interesting design elements, lending character and appeal to the overall result.

Texture and thickness vary with growing conditions, the length of time the gourd remains on the vine, and the gourd's variety—and the range is extreme. Some varieties, such as apple and cannonball, naturally have shells that are not very thick, but extremely hard and dense. Other varieties, such as the canteen and bushel basket, are more likely to have thick shells. Some gourds have dense, resinous shells, while others are soft and porous. These factors will affect how the surface reacts to carving, dying, and other finishing techniques.

Bins of dried gourds, ready for cleaning and crafting. Photo courtesy of Wuertz Farm.

With experience, you'll have more success choosing a gourd that meets your needs. Weight, coloration, and shape offer clues to the crafting characteristics of a particular gourd. However, just as in selecting a melon at the grocery store, even the most experienced gourd crafter is sometimes surprised when the gourd is opened.

SAFETY AND HEALTH CONSIDERATIONS

There are certain hazards associated with dust and mold, and the gourd crafter unfamiliar with them may fall victim to the dreaded "gourd flu." Dust and mold can cause serious respiratory illnesses; their effect is cumulative and may worsen over time. People with allergies or sensitivities may have even more serious consequences if they ignore basic safety considerations. Frequent or repeated exposure to airborne health hazards can create long-term health threats.

Use a good dust mask or respirator rated for protection against toxic or harmful dust. Do not buy inexpensive paper masks labeled "comfort masks"; these do not provide adequate protection. Disposable dust-mask style of respirators are readily available at most hardware stores and are not expensive. Look for a mask with two straps to ensure a more secure seal around the nose and mouth, and read the enclosed instructions to ensure a good fit. Replace disposable dust masks regularly or as they become dirty; they will perform better and last longer if stored in the original packaging or a large zipper-locked plastic bag between uses. If you wear glasses, consider spending a few dollars more to purchase a mask with an exhalation valve. The centralized valve will allow air to flow out of the mask easily during exhalation, instead of forcing it out around the edges of the mask, where it may fog eyeglasses. If you are able to smell gourd dust or molds while you are wearing a mask, the mask is not providing good protection.

A half-face respirator is a better choice if you are sensitive to dust and mold, and require even greater protection. This type of respirator usually has large canister-shaped filters and a soft, tight-sealing rubber mask. The canisters have disposable filters—change them regularly. An added bonus with this type of respirator is that, in some cases, interchangeable filters may be available for fumes from smoke, solvents, and aerosols. Be sure to choose the correct filters: those specific to the types of materials you want to filter. Take time to fit the mask properly so it will seal around your face. No air should escape around the edges of this type of respirator; if you have facial hair, it will hinder creating a good seal.

Be sure to protect your ears if you use power tools for any length of time. Continued exposure to noise in excess of 90 decibels is sufficient to begin a hearing loss, and power tools often run in excess of 100 decibels. Find disposable foam ear protection at hardware stores at minimal cost. The cost of reusable silicone rubber earplugs is slightly higher, and earmuffs designed for industrial use are a bit more.

Keep eye protection in mind, too, when using power tools or creating dust. Regular eyeglasses offer a moderate level of protection, but safety glasses are better; usually shatterproof, they have side seals for closer-fitting protection against flying debris.

Use rubber household gloves or disposable latex gloves when applying messy colorants, such as leather dyes or stains. Latex gloves are low in cost and offer good protection, as long as the thin material is not torn or pierced. Change the glove immediately if it develops a hole, or simply pull on a second glove over the first. Confirm beforehand that you're not allergic to latex; the allergy is very common.

Always use the appropriate safety equipment when working on gourds. Good quality masks and respirators will protect you from exposure to dust and mold. Safety glasses and earplugs protect your eyes and ears when operating power tools.

One hot summer day, I got a frantic call from a gourd-crafting friend, asking how to remove blue leather dye from skin. She had been in a hurry and neglected to place the dye bottle in a mug or safety container. In a clumsy moment, the bottle's contents fell on her bare legs, and despite her best efforts, it remained there until it wore off days later. Don't let carelessness or haste cause accidents.

The most important safety device is common sense. Exercise care and pay attention when using tools and working on gourds. Avoid loose-fitting clothing and hair hanging free; machinery may catch and entangle them, and

Ripples and Streams.

cause injury. Practice care when using sharp knives and gouges. Above all, be aware of opportunities for accidents and use common sense to prevent them. Protect your lungs, eyes, and hands so you can create beautiful works of art for years to come.

Setting Up a Work Area

In a perfect world, everyone would have an unlimited budget and plenty of space to set up the ideal workshop. In reality, most people use a cleaned-off spot on the kitchen counter, a tiny corner of the garage, or a small table parked in front of the television as their work area. Individual needs and available space will make every workshop unique. If space is at a premium, set up small work areas in different locations: use a small nook inside for painting, a corner of the back porch for cleaning, and other areas for storage.

Whether or not you have the luxury of setting up a permanent studio or work area, take some time to lay things out logically. Group like with like, close to the area where the items will most often be used. Keep together tools or items with a similar purpose. Store all cleaning tools in one container, for example. Put paints and painting supplies in an inexpensive storage unit with drawers, and power tools in their own area.

SAFETY IN THE WORK AREA

The most important consideration in choosing a work area is safety. Work outdoors as much as possible to do any cutting or cleaning that creates dust or releases mold spores. This is not always practical, especially in colder climates. If you must do this type of work indoors, it is crucial that the work area be isolated from the main living areas; it must be well ventilated and kept scrupulously clean. Store raw gourds outside at all times so that mold spores cannot filter into living areas.

A dust collection system of some kind is essential to the health of your lungs, whether an exhaust fan, filter, or something else. Buy such items at commercial woodworking stores, or find information on building your own on the Internet. Be aware that, while a dust collection system helps remove some particles from the air, it is an adjunct to a good quality dust mask or respirator, *not* a replacement or substitute.

LIGHTING

Lighting is a big consideration, especially when painting or working with colors. A room facing north with lots of windows is ideal, but hobby lighting that uses a special full-spectrum bulb to produce natural daylight illumination is a good substitute. Create a painting station from any small niche with a work surface, good light, and a bit of storage.

ELECTRICAL

A work area for wood burning, carving, or sawing should have sufficient electrical outlets in close proximity. It poses a possible risk to use long extension cords or operate too many tools from a single outlet. A power strip with several outlets is fine, but be careful not to use several tools at once: this may overload the circuit.

STORAGE

Storage space never seems adequate, no matter how much you have. If space is limited, take some time to organize your tools and supplies so they are easily accessible, but can be stored away neatly when not in use. Clear plastic containers with lids are excellent for most supplies; the contents are visible and the containers can be stacked.

Keep your tools securely stored, safely out of the reach of children. If storing tools outdoors, avoid rust by placing them in a dry area.

Raw gourds can take up a lot of space. Keep them in boxes in the garage or stack them on shelves, or simply leave them outdoors in a pile or in bins. Consider using mesh bags or "toy nets" to hang gourds out of the way when space is at a premium.

Monarch of the Pueblo.
Carved dimensional ripples and faux coiled basketry are a striking backdrop to the monarch butterflies.

Fetish Bear.

2 Gourd-Crafting Basics

Cleaning the Exterior of Green Gourds

Raw gourds have a waxy outer skin that must be removed before the surface is ready for crafting. A gourd that is still green and heavy with moisture is not suitable until it is dried. Gently scrape the skin of green gourds with a paring knife or pocketknife to speed up dehydration. An added benefit to this "green scraping" is the beautiful creamy gourd surface that results.

Because gourds normally dry and cure by a slow process of dehydration, mold will often form on the skin. Green scraping allows moisture to escape rapidly, which limits mold growth. A word of caution: If the gourd is not completely mature when picked from the vine, it may shrivel after green scraping.

Make sure you choose a paring knife with a smooth blade, not a serrated one. A knife with a heavy, solid blade and handle works better than one that is flexible and thin. The blade does not have to be sharp; a slightly dull blade will scrape away the skin rather than cut into the gourd's surface. If you use a pocketknife, a locking blade is safer than one that can accidentally close on your fingers.

To green scrape a gourd, hold the knife so the cutting edge of the blade is almost perpendicular to the gourd surface. Firmly scrape the skin with the blade, making sure to use a scraping and not a cutting motion. The skin should peel easily from the gourd, leaving a beautiful, buttery surface that feels slightly damp. Continue scraping until all the skin is removed. The gourd will dry quickly after this process; the exact time required will vary with ambient air temperature and humidity. If desired, prevent or limit surface molding during the dehydration process by wiping the gourd's surface with a cloth dampened with a mild bleach solution.

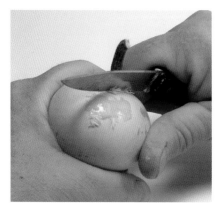

Green scraping a gourd. This technique works best on small gourds and those that are fully mature.

Cleaning the Exterior of Dried Gourds

Moisture is the key to cleaning any dried gourd. A simple scrubbing is often sufficient for gourds grown in areas of high humidity. Prepare a container with warm water; if desired, add a small amount of bleach to the water to kill mold spores. A discarded 5-gallon bucket works well for this purpose, and is easy to clean afterward. Place the gourd in the water and wet the entire surface; cover it with a wet towel while it soaks so the entire gourd remains damp.

The gourd on the left was dried and then cleaned by scrubbing. The gourd on the right was green scraped, producing a clear, light surface without any mold markings.

After soaking, the gourd can be scrubbed to remove the skin and mold.

Gourds grown in dry climates have tough skin that can be hard to remove. If necessary, scrape away the skin first with a dull knife, then finish with a metal scouring pad.

Fine-cutting keyhole saw blades are made to fit a large hobby knife handle.

Use a metal scouring pad (copper or stainless steel) or an abrasive fiber pad to scrub away the dirt, mold, and remaining skin. These inexpensive pads are readily available in most grocery stores, if not your own kitchen. Continue scrubbing to remove all loose surface material. If stubborn spots remain, place the gourd back in the water to soak a bit longer.

For gourds that are tougher to clean, some people suggest using spray-on products meant for oven or heavy household cleaning. While this will certainly work, gourds are relatively easy to clean without resorting to the use of chemicals. Simply increase the length of soaking time for a more resistant gourd by wrapping it in a large, wet towel and placing it in a plastic trash bag. Let the gourd remain in the bag for a few hours or overnight, as needed to soften the waxy skin. Even then, it may be necessary to scrape portions of the gourd with a knife to remove the damp skin. Use the techniques described for green scraping, resoaking, and scraping, as needed. Finish by cleaning the gourd with a metal or fiber scrubber.

Pay attention to the gourd stem during the cleaning process; it often has surface mold and should be scrubbed well. Set aside cleaned gourds to dry completely before painting or decorating.

Cutting a Gourd

BASIC TOOLS AND TECHNIQUES

Many simple tools for gourd crafting are already as close as your kitchen or garage. If you are just beginning, it is wise to use these readily available items. You can always add tools as needed if you choose to continue working with gourds.

Among the tools that are both accessible and easy to use, hobby knives are indispensable and inexpensive. There are many handle and blade styles to choose from, and blades are easy to replace as they become dull or the tips break. Sharp, straight blades are useful for cutting small slits in preparation for sawing a lid or design. Consider using small, keyhole saw blades; these long, thin blades are available to fit heavy-duty hobby knife handles and, with practice, work well for straight cuts, as well as curves.

When cutting with a keyhole saw, begin by stabilizing the gourd on a foam pad, or hold it firmly between your knees. A rubber shelf liner or foam pad will hold the gourd steady and provide some protection against accidental cuts. Pierce the cutting line on the gourd shell with an awl, or make a small starter slit with a sharp hobby blade.

Beginning with a slit instead of a hole will leave no visible starting mark; this is especially suitable for cutting a lid. Place the tip of the pointed blade on the line where you wish to make the cut, pushing slightly to seat it in the gourd. Rock the knife back and forth along the line until it pierces the gourd shell. Then insert the keyhole saw blade into the slit and cut along the marked line.

A full-size handsaw is effective for making straight cuts and removing the tops of gourds, when fit with the appropriate blade. The most important consideration when selecting a blade is the number of teeth per inch. For the smoothest cut, choose a saw blade with fine, closely spaced teeth. The cutting action of a saw produces a narrow gap, or "kerf," as the blade removes material from the cut. Some saw blades are wavy looking or have teeth that are "set" or widely bent, alternating to the right and left. Avoid this type of blade: it cuts a wide kerf. Choose a blade that has tapered teeth with little outward set to the teeth.

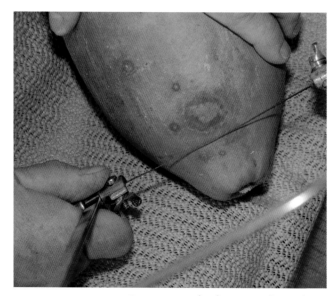

Coping saws, hacksaws, and woodworking crosscut saws are handy when power tools are unavailable. Place the gourd on a foam pad or other non-slip surface during cutting for maximum safety and convenience.

Place the gourd on a firm surface and use a bunched-up towel, foam pad, or rubber shelf liner to provide stability. It may even be helpful to have an assistant hold the gourd during cutting, since the gourd's round shape makes it difficult to stabilize. Begin the cut with a few light pull strokes; then cut the rest of the way with a firm, steady back-and-forth motion. Proceed very slowly and carefully as you near the end of the cut, so as not to crack or chip the gourd as you complete the cut.

SMOOTHING THE CUT EDGE

Smooth and level all cut edges as necessary. A nicely finished edge will give the completed project a neater look. Shape the cut edge with hand files to remove small, inadvertent cut marks and dings, and finish the smoothing process with sandpaper.

Files are indispensable for leveling and flattening cut edges, and are useful for rounding and smoothing the inside edge of a cut gourd. Woodworking hand files are available in different shapes, cuts, and coarsenesses; choose one that is appropriate for the job.

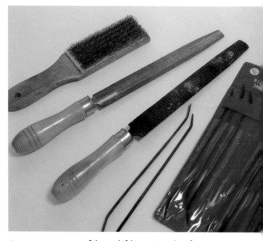

An assortment of hand files. On the far left is a "file card," used to clean files.

A woodworking rasp differs from other files: it has large individual teeth. Use this type of file for quick removal of large amounts of material. Use care when filing with a rasp of any kind; this tool cuts very aggressively and leaves coarse markings that will need to be refined later.

Most woodworking files are "double cut," with two sets of diagonal teeth. File coarseness varies from smooth cut (the finest) to second cut (medium) to bastard (the coarsest). Wooden handles are available for most files and will

Sanding a gourd.

make the file more comfortable to use. I have found that one of the most versatile files for gourd crafting is a half-round, double-cut bastard file. This file has both flat and curved sides, and it cuts aggressively, while leaving a smooth finish.

Use a file card or brush as needed to clean debris from your files; this will keep them cutting more cleanly and smoothly. The file card is a wooden paddle with bristle-like, steel wire teeth. Some file cards also have a brush on the other side for cleaning rasps and removing light debris.

Sandpaper is available in a wide variety of materials and grits, or coarsenesses. Sanding can be tedious at times, but careful attention to this step can mean the difference between a professional-looking project and a sloppy one. Later chapters will explore power-sanding options, but hand sanding will always be necessary when working on curved surfaces such as those of gourds.

TIP: When tearing sandpaper into strips, lay it under a hacksaw blade and pull up to tear. This will give an even edge without dulling your scissors.

It is best to keep sandpaper in a variety of grits on hand, from 80 (medium) to 240 (very fine). Open-coat aluminum oxide sandpaper is a good choice for gourd work; it's less likely to clog with gourd dust and is more durable than inexpensive garnet paper. Sanding sponges are also a good choice for use on gourds; their soft, flexible backing contours to the rounded shape of the gourd.

For best results, begin with one of the coarser grits and switch to finer grits as the work progresses. Increasingly finer grades of sandpaper will eliminate the scratches from previous coarser ones.

Cleaning the Gourd Interior

Opening a cut gourd will reveal a mass of pulp and seeds. This mixture will also have a high concentration of mold, so it is always important to use adequate dust protection when cleaning gourds. If desired, separate the seeds from the pulp and retain them for planting or for use as decorative accent material. The pulp may also be set aside to use in creating gourd paper.

Sometimes it's unnecessary to clean the inside of a gourd. Some people prefer the natural look of the silky white pulp that remains after removing the seeds. For a gourd birdhouse, leave the interior in its natural state; the birds will use the pulp and seed material for nesting.

Many commonly found items are useful for cleaning the gourd interior. Grapefruit spoons, seashells, and canning jar lids work very well and are often on hand. Homemade scrapers are as varied as the people who make them. Bend a hacksaw blade into a shallow loop and fasten it to a wooden handle, using a hose clamp (easily found at any auto supply or hardware store). Sharpen a large, flat washer with a file or grinder, and fasten it to the top of a handle with a large screw. Make some handles with a crook or bend to make it easy to get into those hard-to-reach areas.

Homemade cleaning tools include hacksaw blades, washers, and small router blades, set on homemade handles.

Commercially made tools come in great variety and most are inexpensive. Find ceramic cleaning tools in ceramic or art supply stores; they come in several sizes and shapes. They consist of a wooden handle with a sharpened strip of metal shaped into a loop. Taxidermy fleshing tools are also useful and are available in a variety of shapes and sizes. They have a metal blade with both smooth and serrated edges, and are available from taxidermy and gourd tool suppliers. A pet "shedding brush," easily found at discount and pet stores, has a large metal loop with a serrated edge.

Use any of these tools to scrape the soft fibrous pulp from the gourd interior. Finish by sanding with coarse sandpaper, as needed. Remove as much pulp as possible if the interior is to be painted or colored; the pulp will absorb the color differently from the surrounding cleaned areas. Finish cleaning the gourd interior by removing the small "nipple" that protrudes from the blossom end of the gourd. Use a pair of pliers to pinch and twist off the sharp nipple, then smooth the area.

Design Tools and Techniques

A pleasing gourd project begins with good design and layout. The poorly planned or executed layout of a pattern or its cutting lines may detract from the final product overall, no matter how masterful the rest of the work. Simple techniques will make this process easier and they require few or no tools.

Commercial cleaning tools include taxidermy fleshing tools (upper two) and ceramic cleaning tools (lower two).

MARKING A CIRCLE

You will often need to mark cutting lines or lay out part of a design by drawing one or more circles around the gourd's circumference. Without a specific design reason to do otherwise, you will most often want this line to be level and straight.

Potters use a revolving wheel to help create level bands around their clay forms. In a similar process, you can rotate the gourd by hand to draw a simple

A basic method for drawing level lines around a gourd.

band. Stack a number of flat objects such as books or boards next to the gourd. Continue stacking the objects until they reach the height of the desired line. Place a pencil or other marking tool on top of the stack, extending out so the tip contacts the gourd's surface. To mark the line, hold the pencil firmly atop the stack while rotating the gourd against the pencil tip.

Another method is to place a bowl, glass, or other cylindrical object against the gourd surface and trace around it. A simple compass—available at any store selling school or office supplies—is an inexpensive but valuable tool for drawing circles of any size. In your basic toolbox, you'll find a compass helpful, even indispensable.

SIMPLE GOURD DIVISIONS

For some designs, you will need to divide the gourd accurately into equal sections. Even if high school math was never your strong suit, making reasonably accurate divisions around a gourd is not difficult. Place a strip of masking tape around the circumference of the gourd, trimming the tape so the two ends meet (quilter's marking tape works great for this because it's extremely narrow). Remove the tape carefully, and fold the non-sticky sides together to make equal halves. Make a mark at the fold and, if you require additional sections, continue to fold and mark the tape until you have the appropriate number of sections. Replace the tape on the gourd surface and transfer the marks.

TRANSFERRING PATTERNS

Transferring a flat pattern onto a round gourd may prove an interesting challenge. It may require adjusting the pattern slightly after transferring it, to correct distortions introduced by the gourd's three-dimensional surface. Copy the pattern first onto tracing paper; then use your creativity to customize it before transferring. Your alterations to the pattern will make the completed design more creative and individual.

The most obvious and easy way to transfer a design is to tape a piece of fresh carbon or graphite paper on the gourd surface, tape the pattern over this, and trace the design. Graphite paper is preferred to carbon; carbon paper produces an oily residue that may bleed through paint if not thoroughly removed. White dressmaker's carbon paper is great for making visible lines on very dark gourd surfaces.

If graphite paper is unavailable, cover the back of your pattern with heavy pencil rubbings or chalk. When you place the pattern on the gourd and trace the design, the rubbings will transfer to the gourd surface.

In a pinch, use newspaper as a carbon paper substitute. Select an area densely coated with print, and tape it face down on the surface of the gourd. Place the pattern over this and make the tracing. Lines may be faint or incomplete with this process because only the inked areas will leave a mark; connect the lines with a pencil afterward, if necessary.

You can also transfer patterns from photocopies and laser prints (ink-jet printer copies will not work.). Tape the photocopy face down on the gourd and rub the back of the paper with a hot, DRY iron or commercial transfer tool. The heat from the iron will cause the ink to lift from the surface of the paper and transfer to the gourd surface. Keep in mind that this method will produce a mirror image of the original. Use a photocopier to resize the pattern, as needed. Achieve a similar transfer effect by rubbing a solvent such as acetone over the back of the photocopy. Use this method with caution: the solvent is highly flammable.

Using plastic food wrap may eliminate some of the problems in transferring a flat pattern to a curved surface. Tape a large piece of plastic wrap over the pattern and trace the design on the wrap with a fine permanent marker. Next, tape transfer paper to the gourd and place the plastic wrap over it. Pull snugly and tape the plastic wrap in place; it will contour to the shape of the gourd during the transfer process. Use care to avoid tearing the plastic during the transfer. A ballpoint pen or slightly dull pencil is less likely to tear the wrap.

If the design is to be wood burned, consider using pyrography paper to transfer the pattern. This specially treated translucent paper allows you to burn directly through it into the gourd surface. Simply tape the paper with the design to the gourd, and burn all the lines. A similar method uses a small piece of glass. Lay the glass over the pattern and completely cover it with neatly overlapping strips of masking tape. Be sure the pattern shows through the tape clearly enough to allow for tracing. Trace the pattern on the masking tape, then peel the tape from the glass surface and press it onto the gourd. The tape will conform to the gourd's shape and you can burn the design through the tape.

When the design is complete, remove any stray pencil marks with baby wipes or a damp paper towel. This will remove the pencil lead far more efficiently than a pencil eraser.

A design that has been transferred onto a gourd.

3 Advanced Tools and Techniques

The previous chapter discussed basic hand tools used in gourd crafting. These simple tools are perfectly adequate at first, but after designing a few gourds, you may enjoy finding easier ways to cut, carve, and decorate your master-pieces. This chapter looks at some of the power and specialty tools that make gourd crafting easier, faster, and more enjoyable.

Any discussion of power tools must begin with safety in operating them. Here are a few of the most obvious and essential caveats.

1. Don't wear loose clothing that may become entangled in the tool.
2. Tighten the collet nut or chuck securely before using a new bit.
3. Never start the tool with the bit touching the work surface.
4. Use the side of the cutter, never the tip, for safe and effective cutting. The tip cuts poorly and will chatter on the surface of the gourd, which may damage the gourd and even cause injury.

5. Always be aware of where you hold the rotary tool, relative to your body and your other hand. Rotate the gourd away from you while you cut rather than bringing the power tool closer to your body.

6. Use caution when changing burs: they can build up heat while carving. Burs may be too hot to handle right away with bare hands.

7. Always stay alert when working with power tools. Carelessness and distraction are the foremost causes of injury.

8. Power tools range from the smallest micro saw to the most powerful wood burner, and their price range is equally great. If you're able to attend a gourd show, take the opportunity to try some of the tools for sale there. Some more specialized tools are not widely available—many being offered only at craft shows, on the Internet, or through mail order. Read the owner's manual thoroughly after selecting and buying a tool, so you will fully understand how it works.

Full-Size Power Tools

Full-size jigsaws, band saws, and table-mounted belt or disc sanders are woodworking tools that you might occasionally find useful if they are already in your home workshop. Exercise extreme caution when using any full-size power tool; it will be difficult to control on the rounded shape of a gourd.

A belt sander is very useful for flattening the bottom of a gourd so it sits on the level. Hold the gourd firmly to prevent accidents and damage to the gourd. Table-mounted belt sanders are the safest; if you must use a handheld belt sander, do so only with extreme caution and with the help of an assistant. Take care when sanding the bottom of a gourd; it is easy to sand all the way through inadvertently and create an unwanted hole.

A full-size table-mounted belt sander easily flattens the bottom of a gourd. Be sure to use it with care.

A power drill, which you may already have in your garage or toolbox, can make it easy to clean the most stubborn gourd interior. The safest and easiest drill to use is a variable-speed drill, and the cordless model is preferred. If you already own some other type, try it out before you rush to buy a new one.

Wire brushes and bit extenders are wonderful drill accessories for cleaning the pulp residue from the gourd interior. You can find both items at any hardware store, and the brushes come in an assortment of shapes and textures. Begin with coarse and fine cup-shape brushes in one or two sizes.

Sticks 'n' Stones, Cindy Lee (opposite page, bottom).

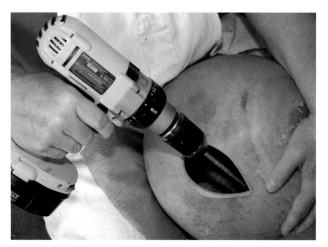

A cordless drill with an attached gourd-cleaning accessory makes short work of cleaning the gourd interior.

Drill bit extenders come in 6- and 12-inch (15- and 30-cm) lengths; these will make it possible to reach the bottom of the tallest gourds. Flap sanding wheels made from abrasive fiber and other drill accessories are handy for smoothing gourd interiors.

There are also specialized gourd-cleaning tools for use in power drills. These include heavy-duty plastic cutting cords and a cement-like ball on a metal extender. Such specialized tools must be mail ordered or purchased at shows, but their particular design makes them priceless additions to the gourd crafter's toolbox.

It is important to maintain a firm grip on both the gourd and the drill when using any accessory to clean out the gourd's inner pulp. Sit in a chair; lay a sheet of rubberized shelf liner across your lap, and grip the gourd firmly between your legs. This will enable you to hold the gourd securely, with both hands free to grasp and steady the drill. Use the drill at the slowest speed setting for the most control; the pressure placed on the drill trigger usually determines the speed. Empty the loosened pulp from the gourd shell frequently, and continue until the interior is clean. If you like, do a final sanding by hand or with a fiber pad attachment.

Cutting Tools

Several manufacturers have developed small hobby-size power saws and other power tools that are ideal for gourd crafting. In my first year at this pursuit, I made all my cuts with either a handheld keyhole saw or a full-size jigsaw. Eventually I discovered that these hobby-size power tools do the same job much more easily and neatly. Now I can't imagine working without them.

Hobby-size saws are available from several different manufacturers, and each has its advantages and drawbacks. All of these saws operate by means of a small transformer. Adapter cords make it possible to connect tools and transformers from different manufacturers, when needed.

The main considerations when purchasing a small saw are the sizes of the saw body and blade, and the shape of the saw foot. Generally, smaller saws with finer blades will handle intricate cuts with ease, while larger saws with heavier blades work better on very thick gourds. Small craft saws are available with flat or ball feet. Many gourd crafters prefer the extra maneuverability, visibility, and control that the ball-shape foot delivers.

If possible, visit a gourd show or retailer and test several saws before you decide which is right for you. If these tools are not available locally, order them on the Internet, or through specialty hobby stores or gourd supply vendors.

To begin cutting an opening or design with a small power saw, first make a starter hole with a hobby blade or awl. When starting to cut a lid, always use a knife to make a starter slit; unlike the round hole made by a drill or awl, this small slit will not show when the cut is completed.

With the power saw turned off, push the saw blade through the starter hole until the foot of the saw is resting firmly against the gourd shell.

Handheld mini-jigsaws like these operate by means of transformers.

Turn on the saw and proceed to cut along the predetermined line. Do not force the saw—let the natural cutting action of the blade do the work. When you reach a gentle curve, simply rotate the saw slightly while the tool continues to run. It may take a bit of practice before you can make accurate and flowing cuts; save gourd scraps to practice on until the cutting operation feels comfortable. When a very sharp change of direction is needed, stop the cut and use a knife to make another starter slit in the new direction. Always turn off the saw before pulling it away from the gourd; this will prevent injury to you and accidental damage to the gourd shell.

Carving Tools

Hand tools alone cannot achieve the superb gourd carving that power rotary tools make possible. All the myriad brands and types of rotary tools available operate similarly.

Transformers come in several types. Verify that your tools and transformers are compatible.

When possible, select a tool that offers variable speeds. Some accessories work best at high speed while others work most efficiently at lower speed; variable speed tools allow you to select the best for each.

Rotary tools are available in cordless and plug-in models. Cordless tools are more portable and have no cords to tangle up or inhibit movement, but lack the power and stamina of plug-in models. A cordless tool also requires frequent battery recharging.

Of the rotary tools pictured, the smaller two on the right work with a transformer and have less power.

Some tools have an optional flex shaft that makes the tool easier to handle, especially for crafters with smaller hands. The flex shaft will feel much cooler during operation because the cutting head is separate from the motor body. It is important to keep the flex shaft as straight as possible during operation. Any extreme bending or torque on the flex shaft will either damage the inner cable or cause the tool to shut off automatically. Suspend the motor body of the tool out of the way from an overhead hook to help keep the flex shaft straight during operation.

Many rotary tool manufacturers offer an optional keyless chuck. This eliminates the need for a wrench and for changing collets when using accessories of different sizes. I highly recommend this to save time and frustration.

> **TIP:** If you don't have a keyless chuck, visit a hobby shop and purchase some ⅛-inch (3-mm) brass tubing. Tubing of this size has the appropriate inside diameter to slide over the shaft of smaller, ³⁄₃₂-inch (2.4-mm) shaft accessories. (It may also be possible to find reasonably close-fitting tubing for metric burs.) Cut pieces to the appropriate length and use superglue or solder to fasten them securely to the shafts of each accessory. These adapted burs eliminate changing collets. Some manufacturers also offer "collet adapters," which make it possible to use burs of different sizes without changing collets.

This heavy-duty rotary tool uses a flex shaft and a variety of handpieces.

Select the tool most appropriate for your needs. For carving tools that you expect to use infrequently, almost any type will do. If carving appeals to you, however, consider purchasing a high quality, heavy-duty tool that will offer years of superior performance.

CARVING BURS

Rotary tools are extremely versatile when you have a variety of accessories and cutting burs available, and a great variety of burs and accessories are suitable for carving. After many years of crafting, I find that I routinely use certain favorites—the rest of them sit idle, except for very specific cutting or carving operations. A large investment in burs and accessories is therefore needless for the beginning carver. Making most of the projects in this book called for four or five basic burs.

The carving burs on the left are structured tooth carbide burs; those on the right are high-speed steel cutters.

A familiarity with the types of carving burs makes it easier to select the proper ones for different applications. Experiment with a variety of burs to find which you prefer for each step of carving.

Structured tooth carbide burs are invaluable for initial roughing; the unique design of these burs makes them ideal for cutting large areas smoothly and quickly. Structured tooth burs are a bit unusual in appearance, with tiny, needle-like teeth projecting from the surface. The spacing of the teeth minimizes clogging or "loading," which allows the bur to cut efficiently. This type of bur is available in a wide range of shapes and sizes, and often in fine to extremely coarse cutting grits. The very small cutting teeth of the finer carbide burs produce a smooth cut with only a slight textured pattern. This texture can nicely simulate fur, in lieu of more laborious burning techniques.

Because these burs are considered woodworking specialty items, they are not widely marketed. You find them most often at woodworking stores or other outlets that cater to wood-carvers. Marketed under several brand names, these burs vary in color and appearance. For gourds, use burs that are silver or gold; these are of fine to medium coarseness and cut smoothly without excessive tearing or gouging. Burs of other colors are not as well suited to gourds; they are much coarser and cut quite aggressively.

Structured tooth burs in three or four different shapes are probably all you need for most gourd carving. Each shape has certain qualities that make it better for specific carving operations. Select at least one bur with a flat end, for example, a cylinder or inverted cone. The edge at the tip of the bur is great for cutting sharp, clean lines, such as the edge of a border, and the flat side effectively smoothes large areas.

Choose another bur with a rounded body or tip, such as a ball or ball-nosed shape, for removing material where you want no sharp edges. This bur's rounded shape quickly cleans out large areas, leaving no noticeable lines.

Finally, select a bur with a pointed tip, such as a long taper or flame shape. The tip carves well in tight areas, while the side of the bur nicely rounds and refines shapes

High-speed steel cutters have many shaping and cutting applications, and their low cost makes them especially appropriate for beginning carvers. Outlets that sell rotary tools and accessories generally carry steel cutters in numerous shapes, sizes, and shaft diameters. The more common midrange shaft sizes are the most appropriate for rotary tools. Generally, heavy-duty cutting burs will have a thicker shaft, while those for fine detail carving have a thinner shaft.

Use steel cutters of shapes similar to structured tooth carbide burs in the same manner as described above. Some steel cutters are designed for

A ball-shape bur is used to cut a recessed area into which a decorative piece of glass will fit.

On this gourd, small dots are being carved for decoration.

specialty applications, such as inlay, texturing, and line engraving. Among them are wheel-shape burs, which are extremely useful for cutting slots and sharply defined lines. Use small ball-shape burs for stippling or texturing backgrounds, and small steel engraving cutters for fine detail renderings and carving in hard-to-reach areas.

Don't use diamond burs for cutting through the tough outer gourd skin; their very fine cutting grit makes them effective only on the gourd's inner "meat." Diamond burs work best for fine texturing or attaining a smooth finish with minimal removal of material. The finely spaced grit of diamond burs makes them more likely to clog than other burs; they require frequent cleaning to maintain their cutting surface.

Most rotary tool packages include bit accessories, such as sanding drums. With replaceable bands of fine or coarse sandpaper, the drums quickly sand and smooth large areas. Take the time to loosen the screw on the top of the sanding drum occasionally, pull the band up slightly, and retighten. This adjustment provides a sharp cutting edge at the top of the band, and shields the screw from accidentally marring the carving surface. Replace worn or clogged bands by loosening the screw and sliding the sanding bands on and off the drum.

The Mechanics of Carving

Maintain a good, solid grip on both the gourd and the carving tool. Work with the gourd held firmly in your lap. A large piece of rubberized shelf liner provides a good non-slip surface; for convenience, sew a piece of this material to the front of your work apron. Hold the gourd with one hand and use the other to grasp the tool. Keep a firm grip on both the tool and the gourd at all times.

Most people instinctively pick up a rotary tool and hold it like a pencil. This type of grip suits fine detail work, but heavy or aggressive carving requires a grip with better control. The pencil grip will quickly fatigue your hand, especially with a full-size rotary tool or large handpiece.

The "power grip" is the most secure and ergonomic; hold the tool under the palm of your hand similarly to grasping a paring knife or potato peeler. The weight of the tool below the hand causes less fatigue than the pencil grip. Rest the side of your thumb against the gourd and use it as an anchor to steady and guide the hand as you carve. The index and middle finger knuckles serve as secondary resting and guiding points for extra stability.

Be aware of the direction in which the bur rotates. The direction in which the dust and chips are thrown indicate which way the tool is spinning. The

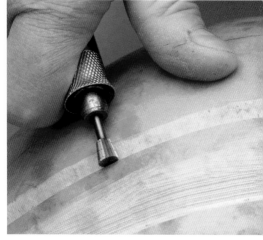

The "power grip."

tool will cut most aggressively and with the best control when drawn in the same direction as the bur's spin. Right-handed carvers have the most control when drawing the tool toward them, or rotating the gourd away. Used in the opposite direction, the bur may climb out of the cut and cause injury.

For safety, if you're right-handed, develop the habit of rotating the gourd away as you work, rather than drawing in your carving hand too closely. This keeps the tool a safe distance from your body, and away from the other hand holding the gourd. It may sound a bit complicated, but it feels very natural with just a little practice.

Left-handed carvers face some additional challenges, as the cutting edges on many steel burs are unidirectional and are designed for right-handed applications. Some burs, such as diamonds and structured tooth carbide burs, are without directional flutes, and work more efficiently for left-handed operators.

These mini power sanders are powered by transformers. From left to right, they are a pad sander, disc sander, and belt sander. Front, a mini pad sander.

Sanding and Grinding Tools

There are many sanding accessories available for use in rotary tools. Drum and disc sanders come in different sizes and grits, and are great for quick sanding jobs. You can find small hobby-size power sanders and grinders in several styles, including belt sanders, disc sanders, and small detail sanders. Manufactured by the same companies that produce many of the small saws, these tools will operate with the same transformers. The small belt sander is handy for smoothing the bottom of a gourd, shaping gourd pieces for jewelry, and sanding cut edges. The small disc sander works extremely well for grinding resin inlay. Your own personal preferences and the techniques you most commonly use will ultimately determine the value of any tool in your arsenal.

General Tool Operation

If you are fortunate enough to own a variable speed tool, take full advantage of it. Most bur packaging indicates the maximum safe speed recommended by the manufacturer. Be sure to take notice if you have a bur rated at a lower speed than your tool can deliver. A bur can disintegrate when used at excessive speed, possibly causing serious injury.

In general, steel and carbide cutters work most effectively at higher speeds. Experiment with different speeds to reduce the "chattering," or bouncing of the bur on the gourd surface.

Operate sanding drums at a reduced speed. High speeds can make the sanding abrasive clog, and even burn the gourd surface from excess friction. At high speed, the outsized head of a sanding drum creates a lot of torque, possibly enough to bend the shaft, and cause the tool to wobble.

Insert the shaft fully into the collet or chuck to avoid damage to the bur or accessory. Seat the bit fully, and then back it out slightly to ensure the shaft is adequately supported. Always remember to tighten the chuck firmly when changing burs.

Gourds naturally contain resins, which can clog the bur and reduce its cutting ability. Keep burs clean and free of residue for best operation. Clean structured tooth carbide burs by flaming with a propane torch; immerse other burs in a jar of solvent, or spray them with oven cleaning products. With care, most burs last a long time.

Burning Tools—Pyrography

Burning decorative designs into wood, leather, and gourds is an ancient art. Some cultures still use simple sticks with glowing embers, and even with these crude instruments, achieve beautiful designs. Modern enthusiasts gave the craft the more scientific-sounding name "pyrography," literally meaning "fire writing."

There are two basic styles of pyrography tool: a self-contained tool styled like a soldering iron with a heavy tip, and one comprising a transformer and a burning pen with a fine wire tip. Both work well on gourds and have a variety of tip styles.

The soldering-iron style of burner looks like a large fat pen with a power cord attached. A heat-resistant material protects the handle, and a flared finger guard keeps your hand away from the hot tip. Found in many craft stores, these inexpensive burners are often the first ones that gourd crafters purchase. With their extensive variety of optional screw-in tips, they are handy for burning simple decorative patterns. A drawback to the soldering-iron burner is that its design permits less control, your hand being at a distance from the burning tip. This burner also transfers heat less efficiently, so it is slower to heat and to recover heat between strokes. While its low price makes it suitable for the beginner, more advanced gourders usually prefer the comfort and control of a transformer-style burner.

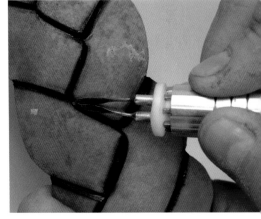

The use of a wood burner can add shading and depth to a piece.

The transformer-and-pen burner has a power supply with a rheostat to control heat output and is available in a vast array of sizes and shapes. All the many brands of plug-in transformer units work pretty well, so base your selection on price, handpiece style and size, comfort, and your own personal preference.

Professional-quality tools like these transformer-unit burners permit the use of a variety of burning pens and tips.

There are other things important to consider when purchasing burning pens, such as whether to buy a fixed-tip handpiece or one with interchangeable tips. The latter are a little less expensive (as you are buying only one handpiece and several tips), but they have a major drawback: Replaceable tips are prone to loosen during burning. The resulting intermittent conduction can cause the handle of the unit to heat up, and the pen to burn inefficiently. Some brands of interchangeable-tip pens are reasonably good, but if you can afford it, a fixed-tip handpiece is a better choice.

Some manufacturers offer a choice between heavy-duty or regular pens and cords, and other options, including heavy-duty and vented handpieces, and optional foam and rubber coverings to make them more comfortable to use. If you are doing heavy, deep burning, you may be better off with heavy-duty pens and cords, vented handpieces, and protective handpiece coverings. For light burning and shading, the lighter weight pens are fine. Pens are sometimes interchangeable among various units with the purchase of optional adapter cords. Once again, trying these out at a show or retailer will enable you to decide more knowledgeably which ones work best for you.

Pyrography pens come in a variety of tip styles. Even self-contained soldering-iron style of pens have many different tips. A dagger or skew shape is good and versatile for lines and general purpose burning. Begin with one of these basic shapes and gradually add specialty tips as needed. Most people find one or two favorites that they use for the majority of their burning.

The five burning pens on the left have fixed tips, while the one on the right has replaceable tips.

For the projects in this book, I used only two tips: a dagger and a ball. The dagger shape is wonderful for burning straight or curved lines, and I use both edges of the tip. When burning residue coats one edge, I simply switch to the other. The ball shape works well for shading large areas, but I also use it for stippling and making decorative dots.

When burning, hold the handpiece at a sufficient angle so the heat from the burning tip rises away from your fingers. Use the side of your hand or your little finger as a fulcrum to steady your hand and provide more control. Practice burning on a few gourd scraps to determine the proper heat setting, one that will give a nice, dark line without excessive drag (meaning the temperature is too low) or dark charring and a profusion of smoke (meaning the temperature is too high). Tend toward lower temperatures until you feel comfortable with the burner; it's easier to go back and darken a burn than to repair an area burned too deeply. Every gourd—sometimes even different areas of the same gourd—will require different heat settings, owing to differences in the density and texture of the shell. Practice and experience will guide you in future projects.

For optimal performance, keep the burning tip clean by occasionally removing any residue that accumulates. Always follow the manufacturer's recommendations for cleaning and sharpening tips.

Final Finishing

While power tools do many things quickly and easily, a few good hand tools finish the job. Use an art or hobby knife with plenty of sharp blades for cleaning up a carving; it does a nice job of undercutting, trimming edges, cutting fine details, and more. Blades are fairly inexpensive; don't hesitate to change them when the tip breaks or the edge dulls. A sharp blade cuts; a dull one tears the fibers of the gourd.

Rifflers are small hand files that are bent at both ends, usually sold in sets with several shapes. They're ideal for smoothing contours, as they get into tight corners impossible to reach with sandpaper or burs. Invaluable tools, rifflers can be hard to find; look for them where woodworking supplies are sold.

Sandpaper of various grits is a necessity for final finishing. Use increasingly fine grades of sandpaper, finishing with the finest grit for the smoothest surface.

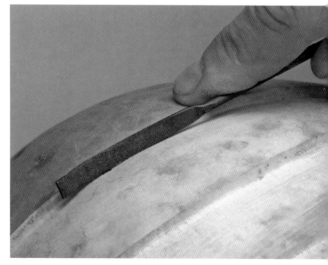

Rifflers are invaluable for sanding and smoothing carved areas.

Specialty Tools

More advanced carvers might want to consider an air-driven rotary tool, which runs at about ten times the speed of an electric rotary tool and operates with a smaller, lighter handpiece. Unlike electric rotary tools, air tools generate very little heat, making it possible to use the tool comfortably for extended periods. Compressed air drives this type of tool and it requires a compressor (or in some cases, carbon dioxide) for operation. Air-driven tools are relatively expensive but well worth the money if you are serious about detailed carving and engraving on gourds.

Similar to dental drills, air-driven rotary handpieces run at extremely high speeds.

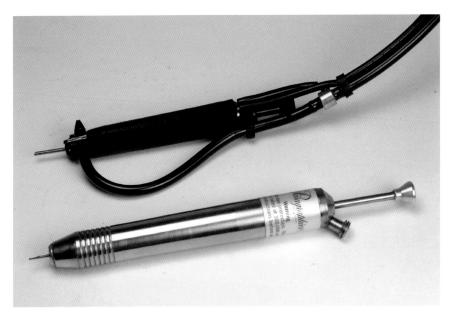

Gourd-Crafting Materials

Today's gourd artists have an enormous wealth of products available to them. Choose the materials that meet your needs and desires, and spend some time experimenting with new ones as you discover them. Don't hesitate to try products you have on hand from other hobbies or projects; almost every art material has some kind of application for gourds.

Coloring Agents

DYES

There are a number of dyes and inks appropriate for use on gourds and most are transparent, often allowing the natural surface of the gourd to show through. Among them are leather dyes, which provide more intense color and generally work better on gourds than fabric dyes. Most leather dyes are

Place the dye bottle inside an old coffee mug to prevent and contain spills. Always wear gloves to protect your hands from stains.

alcohol based and can be thinned with ordinary rubbing alcohol. The major drawback to leather dyes is that many of them are not colorfast and will fade. If you like the look that leather dyes produce, certain steps can minimize—but not eliminate—fading. First, add a capful of vinegar to the bottle of leather dye. The vinegar helps the colors set and reduces future fading. Second, always use a final finish with an ultraviolet ray (UV) protectant on gourds colored with dyes. This will reduce somewhat the effect of the UV rays that cause fading. Finally, as with any other fine work of art, keep the finished gourd out of direct sunlight.

As you use them, keep in mind that leather dyes are formulated for dying leather—and your skin is a form of leather. Always wear gloves to protect your hands. Spilled dyes will permanently stain clothing, furniture, and other porous items. To prevent and contain spills, place opened bottles of dye in a heavy ceramic coffee mug or other suitable holder. Shield your work surface with a layer of newspaper or other absorbent material.

Use disposable brushes, cotton swabs, or cloth pads to apply dyes. You may use the daubers that come with many brands of dye, but don't expect any accuracy with them; they soak up dye quickly and release it just as quickly, often causing runs and drips. Use your chosen applicator with care and thoroughly clean used applicators with rubbing alcohol (or discard them) when you are finished.

The application of dye to gourds.

For loose, free-flowing color washes, some gourd artists use silk dyes over a gesso base, which can produce unusual tie-dye effects in bright colors. Salts of different coarsenesses create interesting effects in the wet dyes.

A product that rubber stamp enthusiasts use with great success is "dye ink." You can buy this colorant as a refill and use it similarly to any other type of dye. The primary advantage of this medium is better colorfastness. Dye inks that are alcohol based retain their color longer than those that are water soluble. Whatever coloring agent you use, always test any new product for color durability before using it on a project.

WAXES AND POLISHES

Shoe polishes have long been used to color and finish gourds, but newer colored waxes and polishes are coming out in a growing range of colors. Various shoe polish colors can be mixed with each other and most other waxes. Apply them with a soft cloth; allow the polish to dry to a dull finish, then buff for a lustrous finish. Gourds finished with these products retain much of the raw gourd's natural feel, and most colors are semitransparent, allowing the gourd shell markings to show through. But be aware that, to maintain the finish, the polish may require occasional reapplication and buffing.

Colored and metallic paste-type waxes are another option, available at craft stores and gourd shows in brand names from several manufacturers. Most of these products are solvent based and require turpentine for cleanup and thinning. You can use a small brush, cotton applicator, soft cloth, or even a finger to apply and spread these waxy pigments. Results will vary depending on skill in application, porosity and texture of the surface to which it's applied, and quality of the product. Use these products in combination with other coloring agents or as an accent. Some artists who use them as their only means of coloration have become quite adept at achieving stunning and distinctive finishes. Use care when selecting the final finish over these products: some materials are incompatible and the finish may degrade over time. Read the labels to determine the proper finish, or whether another finish (than the wax) is even

A gourd teapot painted with metallic coating.

required. (When buffed, some wax coloring agents will develop a shine and a natural protective finish.)

Also suitable for gourds are wood-staining waxes, usually a soft paste that comes in a can or tube, and liquid polishes containing a stain. These can produce a lovely deep shine as they add subtle color. Experiment by applying wax or polish over paint or other material on a gourd scrap. For best results, always ensure beforehand that the products you want to use are compatible. Apply polishes with a soft cloth, laying on a thin, even layer. Let the wax or polish dry to a haze before buffing to a high shine with a clean, soft cloth.

PENCILS, PENS, AND INKS

Colored pencils can be used alone or in combination with pyroengraving, pen and ink, markers, and other materials and methods. There are three different kinds of colored pencil: wax based, oil based, and water soluble, each with its own characteristics. The most common inexpensive colored pencil sets are wax based. You can try them all without significant expense, since many art stores sell pencils individually. Purchase one or two of each type and experiment to see which you prefer; remember that they can all be used together. Be aware of the range within each type of pencil, too: if you compare an inexpensive wax pencil from a child's set to an artist's quality wax pencil, the difference will be obvious.

Colored pencils, inks, and a variety of markers offer alternatives to dyes and paints.

The shade of the natural gourd skin will affect color applied with pencils; pencil colors appear most intense on lighter gourd surfaces. For interesting effects, try blending oil-based pencil colors with a solvent such as turpentine, or water-based colors with water. Erasers are handy for cleaning stray marks. Seal the finished pencil project with a matte fixative to set the colors, and spray it with a final finish for durability.

Both water- and solvent-based marking pens are great for work on gourds. The water-based variety is especially good for children's use. Do keep in mind that subsequent applications of solvent-based finishes may adversely affect the pigments of some marking pens. Always test materials for compatibility.

Artist's colored inks are another option for achieving transparent color effects. These inks come in small bottles and are somewhat expensive, making them unsuitable for shading large areas. Use colored inks with a brush or pen to color fine details.

PAINTS AND STAINS

Paint of almost any kind can be used on gourds, from ordinary house paint to the most expensive artist's-quality oil. Every artist has a variety of favorite products, each with its distinctive qualities suited to different styles and methods. Before painting, some artists like to apply a base coat of gesso to the gourd; this is usually necessary only to mask a very dark surface.

Water-based acrylic paints are by far the most commonly used. They are widely available in a vast range of brands and colors (including metallic, interference or iridescent, and pearlescent), and plain water cleans them easily. Some acrylic paints contain added material to give texture and some are made specifically for outdoor use. Though the choice may be difficult, try to begin with a limited palette of colors and types; you'll be more likely to use them all. You can add others as you need them.

Other options for gourd painting are inexpensive bottled acrylics and traditional tube and other specialty acrylics made specifically for tole painters and other artists. I use bottled craft store acrylics most often when I'm sponge painting or covering large areas. I prefer higher quality artist's acrylics for painting images that require blending or shading. Their colors are more intense, they blend well, and they usually cover better. If you are a novice, try the less expensive acrylic paints first. You can always experiment with the more expensive, better quality acrylics later, and they can all be used interchangeably.

Rufous Hummer.

Painting tools you might want to try include foam and regular brushes, artist's sea sponges, and even a toothbrush.

Oil paints can be messy, but a skilled application can yield deep, lustrous, even dimensional color not possible with most other products. Mix oil paints with turpentine, flow mediums, or linseed oil for use as a stain; this will produce an endless palette of color. Oil paints dry slowly and require turpentine for cleanup of hands and tools. If you already have oil paints on hand, you should certainly try them on your gourds, but many people will find they prefer other products.

Artists preferring a softer, more transparent finish find success with watercolor paints. Use a good quality, lightfast watercolor paint; these are usually available as a paste in small tubes or as a liquid in small bottles.

The transparency of the watercolor will allow burned or inked lines and the gourd shell's natural markings to show through. As with colored pencils, the natural color of the gourd shell will also affect the watercolors' final appearance. For example, because a yellow-toned gourd surface shows through the transparent watercolor medium, a blue shade may end up appearing somewhat greenish. Some artists employ a technique that mixes both watercolors and overlaid oil-based colored pencils. The thin application of a white or lighter-value pencil over a watercolor base often makes the underlying colors brighter and more intense.

Watercolors are also good for staining a gourd's surface. Use watercolor in an ink-like consistency, and apply it with a soft cloth or paper towel. Work quickly to avoid lines and watermarks. Apply shoe cream afterward, if desired, to smooth any marks and add a soft luster to the surface. A final finish of shoe wax or an acrylic spray will provide a further protective coating. If applying shoe wax, use care to avoid rubbing too hard and possibly removing some of the underlying color.

Stains with a base of water, oil, or lacquer also work on gourds, but have certain limitations. The wood stains commonly sold in hardware stores are intended for a more porous surface than gourd skin. These stains will not soak readily into the hard outer gourd shell, but will do so rapidly into areas carved or gouged. The lacquer-based stains available through specialty wood-working stores can produce intense, transparent colors, but are expensive and usually not colorfast.

Lacquer-based spray paints originally developed for use in the floral industry are now commonly sold in craft stores. More transparent than enamel-based sprays, these paints are not suitable for outdoor use. Lacquer-based sprays do nicely for creating decorative effects over acrylic paints, but never use them over enamel-based paints or finishes. If you do use a lacquer-based spray paint, be sure to experiment first on scrap pieces, and be aware of possible compatibility problems.

Other specialty paints and glazes available at art, hobby, and hardware stores are all suitable for gourd art, including patina paints, textural sprays, faux painting glazes, and paints with other additives. The projects will explore some of these.

Colorful bug pins.

Finishing

WAXES AND OILS

Use linseed, tung, mineral, and furniture oils with confidence on gourds, but avoid using kitchen or cooking oils: some of these may turn rancid and sticky over time. Oils penetrate and seal the gourd shell but their absorption depends on the shell's porosity, making them better suited for gourds decorated simply, with a more natural finish. Apply oils with a soft cloth and remove any excess with a second clean cloth. Follow the manufacturer's directions for detailed application. Keep in mind that an oil finish may need periodic reapplications to maintain a soft, creamy surface. Exercise caution when disposing of waste items used to apply the finish: they may be subject to spontaneous combustion.

Colored paste waxes were mentioned earlier, but a number of clear waxes and polishes—including shoe creams and polishes, furniture waxes, floor waxes, and more—may also be applied to gourds. Wax products are generally designed for specific applications and, because a gourd shell is similar to

Nesting Time.
Costa's hummingbirds and eucalyptus.

wood, those waxes intended for fine woods, leather, and hardwood floors are more appropriate for gourds. Those manufactured for use on cars are obviously less suitable. Apply the wax with a soft cloth, allow it to dry to a dull or hazy finish, and buff it to a fine glow.

Among floor finishes available in liquid form, acrylic polymers that dry to a hard, durable finish work well on gourds. Native potters have used this type of finish for years, to add the final sheen to their pieces. The pores of the gourd shell absorb the fluid; reapply as needed until they absorb no more. After that, let the gourd dry and then polish it with a soft cloth to bring out the shine.

FOOD-SAFE PRODUCTS

If you plan to use your gourd for things you will eat or drink, be sure to use a food-safe finish. Natural food-safe materials such as beeswax have long been used to seal and protect water-carrying containers. Other such products developed for woodworking and available through woodworking outlets are also good for this purpose.

One of the oldest and most traditional ways of preparing a gourd for use with water—one used by native cultures since prehistoric times—is to soak and flush it with water repeatedly until the natural bitter taste of the gourd is eliminated. The porous gourd shell allows for evaporation of the liquid, providing a natural cooling effect. To treat a gourd in this manner, fill the gourd with plain or salted tap water, let it sit overnight, and repeat. It may take several soakings to eliminate the bitterness. Some people suggest using other additives such as sugar or baking soda, but plain water does just as well. This process will not seal the gourd shell, but will make liquids stored within taste better.

Use beeswax or paraffin to seal the gourd's interior to prevent evaporation or leakage; beeswax will also add a delightful fragrance. Handle these products with caution: Both must be applied in a hot, liquid state, and paraffin is highly flammable. Wax applied to a cold gourd will not adhere or soak into the shell, and may flake off the surface. Place your cleaned, undecorated gourd in a warm oven while you melt the wax in a double boiler. Use the lowest temperature setting on the oven; the gourd needs to be warmed only enough so that the wax will thoroughly penetrate the shell. (Do not use a microwave: it's harder to control and may damage the gourd shell.) When the wax has fully melted, pour it directly into the shell. Use care to prevent burns or spills; wear protective gloves and work over a surface covered with a layer of newspapers. Rotate the gourd until the interior is evenly coated with wax, and then pour out the excess. Use care to keep the shell's exterior free of wax because paints and other materials will not adhere to it.

You can use different finishes for gourds to hold things other than water. Woodworking stores sell special food-safe products, which are guaranteed to be nontoxic when dry; the easiest to use among them is polyurethane. Oils meant for salad bowls and butcher blocks are also appropriate.

VARNISHES AND SEALERS

Solvent- and water-based sealers and varnishes come in formulas for both brush-on and spray application. Some of them contain additives such as UV protectants and flattening agents.

Varnish is a combination of synthetic resins mixed with drying oils, usually named for the type of resin it contains. Polyurethane, urethane, alkyds, and phenolic varnishes are among this kind. Some varnishes contain oils and are sold as wiping products. In general, varnishes provide a strong, durable finish, but dry slowly.

A substance derived from scale insects and usually dissolved in alcohol, shellac has been used for centuries. It has the advantage of drying quickly, but causes a natural yellowing of the cured finish. Shellac may be used on gourds, but less well than other finishes.

Woodworking professionals favor lacquer, made from cellulose resins and a variety of solvents and binders, for its rapid drying and beautiful depth. A lacquer finish also performs well as a sealer under acrylics: it prevents the raising of gourd fiber on the subsequent application of such water-based paints. Lacquers are not suitable, however, for prolonged exposure outdoors or to moisture, and cannot be used over other solvent-based finishes.

Pronghorn Plains.

Water-based finishes contain some of the same resins as other finishes, without the solvent. These have a much easier water cleanup, but sacrifice some degree of durability. Most water-based finishes are sold as a brush-on, rarely as a spray.

Clear craft sprays and brush-on finishes are extremely suitable for use on gourds and available in acrylic and enamel bases. These products dry quickly, come in a variety of finishes (including gloss, semigloss, and matte), and many offer UV protection, making them the most versatile and widely used finishes for gourd crafting.

Wood hardener is a specialty product originally created to harden and repair rotted wood. It is an epoxy resin in dispersion, readily absorbed by the soft interior surface of a gourd, owing to its liquid state. Poured into or

This butterfly birdhouse needs to be treated with an outdoor-safe finish.

brushed on the gourd surface, the resin will soak deeply into the pores of the shell; as the resin hardens, it adds strength to a thin or soft gourd. When cured, the hardener becomes inert and no longer releases toxins or other chemicals. A variety of brands and formulas are available in both water and solvent bases.

OUTDOOR-SAFE FINISHES

Projects that will be exposed to the elements, such as birdhouses, should first be treated with a wood preservative. For the safety of the bird inhabitants, use a creosote-free product and treat only the outside surfaces. Leave the interior of the gourd untouched. A wood preservative will protect the surface and inhibit the growth of mold or fungus. But this product is not a final finish; use it in conjunction with an appropriate sealer.

Solvent-based finishes such as spar varnish and polyurethane are more durable than those with water bases, and are available in both spray and brush-on forms. Their biggest drawback is their lengthy drying time, and both may yellow when exposed to sunlight. This may not be a problem on items with a natural finish but it may cause the color of painted or decorated gourds to change over time. All finishes should be renewed periodically, depending on conditions in the local environment.

Structural Additives

GLUES AND ADHESIVES

Of the wide variety of glues, adhesives, and filler products on the market, this section will deal with a select group best suited for use on gourds.

White glue (also known as polyvinyl acetate or PVA glue) is water soluble, dries clear and flexible, and is nontoxic. The more viscous, heavy-bodied brands work better for most gourd applications. Keep in mind that white glue can take up to an hour to begin setting and the cured project will not be waterproof.

Yellow glue (also known as aliphatic resin or carpenter's glue) is similar to white glue, but is more resistant to moisture and heat. Yellow glue begins to set more quickly than white glue and is suitable for both indoor and outdoor applications. White and yellow glue will produce the strongest bond when pieces fit tightly and they are clamped or otherwise held in place as the glue cures.

Cyanoacrylate glue (CA or superglue) is extremely useful for quick adhesion or control of application. Gap-filling CA glue—usually available at hobby or train stores—is best for use on gourds; it works better on porous surfaces than the thinner CA glues. (If you can't find this product, check your local hardware store for a gel form of cyanoacrylate glue, which is thicker than normal CA glue.) One advantage of CA glue is that it comes in a small container with a very slender applicator, making it possible to apply the glue accurately in tiny areas. This class of glue is solvent based; use acetone or nail polish remover to clean up or remove the glue from skin. CA glue lasts longer when stored in a cool, dry area.

You can use CA glue in conjunction with other glues. When joining two parts with wood glue, add a tiny drop of CA glue for an instant grab. This will help to hold the pieces together while the wood glue dries to a strong bond.

Epoxy glues might occasionally be useful for limited applications, such as fixing a non-porous stone or other item to a gourd. Some types of epoxy glues may also function as a resin base for inlaying crushed stone.

Construction adhesives are great in situations where you might once have used a hot melt glue gun. Hot melt glue is always a poor choice for gourd art, since it's extremely intolerant of changes in temperature and other environmental factors, and the bond often fails. On the other hand, construction adhesive begins to cure rapidly and forms a strong bond over the following 24 hours. It's available in both a wood color and clear, and is thick enough to stay where you put it. This strong, waterproof adhesive works well for joining dissimilar materials; in fact, it is one of the few adhesives suitable for use on foam. Available at most hardware stores, construction adhesive comes in small project-size tubes or large caulking gun tubes.

An interior of a gourd painted with glue.

WOOD FILLERS

Wood fillers are useful for repairs and construction projects. Use them to fill flaws in the gourd surface or to blend joints. In a pinch, the handiest wood filler is a mixture of gourd dust and glue. Mix the dust into a small amount of white or wood glue to a thick, paste-like consistency. Press this material into crevices for a strong patch. This type of patch may accept stains or dyes, but will often look noticeably different from the surrounding area.

Many common paste or putty wood fillers are cellulose based, and come in both solvent- and water-based formulas. The filler is packaged in tubes, small tubs, or cans. The small tubes are good for infrequent use, since the filler will not dry out as quickly as that in the cans. Water-based fillers are the best for work on gourds, because they are easy to use and clean up. Use fillers in thin layers when the area to be repaired is deep; thinner layers dry more quickly and are less likely to crack. The final layer of filler should overfill the depression a bit because the material shrinks slightly as it dries. The cured filler can be filed, sanded, or carved.

Since many brands of wood filler do not absorb dyes and stains as well as the surrounding gourd surface, it may be necessary to cover the repair with

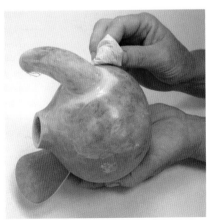

Wood filler is applied around the joints where parts have been added.

acrylic paint or some other coloring agent. Some fillers produced expressly for the craft market may be better in this respect; try different varieties until you find one that meets your needs.

For repairs demanding extra strength, try two-part epoxy wood fillers. This type of filler will not accept stain, but is incredibly strong. This is the best filler for outdoor applications, where the material will be exposed to moisture.

CLAY PRODUCTS

Air-dry clays of many kinds are on the craft market these days, and home-made recipes abound. Clay recipes are often based on flour, cornstarch, and other foodstuff that vermin find attractive, so use them with caution.

Air-dry products dry naturally at room temperature without the need for heat curing. Because these products contain a lot of moisture, they must be kept tightly wrapped or in an airtight container between uses. If they begin to dry out, knead a small amount of water into the clay and return to the airtight container.

A variety of additives provides the base for air-dry clays, including pumice, paper pulp, cellulose, and talc. The exact combination of materials will determine the dry weight of the final product, and its texture and ability to hold fine detail. Every brand of clay has slightly different characteristics; with experience, you'll develop a personal preference.

This type of clay is very versatile, with uses from filler for making patches to the basis for sculptural figures. Create larger sculptured forms by building over a skeleton or framework made from wire, crumpled foil, or gourd parts. Build layers slowly to avoid cracking. Air-dry clay adheres well to gourd surfaces, but for added security, spread a thin layer of white glue on the gourd where you intend to place the clay. When dry, you can sand or carve the material. Color air-dry clay if you like by kneading water-based paint into the wet clay or by painting the clay surface after it has dried.

Polymer clay must be baked in an oven to cure properly. Because the heat required to cure the clay can damage the gourd shell or cause it to become brittle, form the clay and remove it from the gourd prior to baking. Be aware that polymer clay can be sealed only with a water-based finish. Sprays and solvent-based finishes will react with the clay and make the surface permanently sticky or gummy. Though it can be used on gourds, these drawbacks make polymer clay more difficult to work with and less versatile than air-dry.

The projects in Part Two are arranged in order of difficulty; you may find some of the later projects more challenging. Each project introduces a new skill, technique, or material, and the later projects draw on techniques and useful information in earlier projects. You may want to review certain details as necessary.

A gourd coated with a thin layer of paper clay.

Southwestern Gourd Designs

PETROGLYPH POTTERY

Primitive peoples created art on rock walls that continues to captivate modern viewers. Create your own rock art on a gourd, using acrylic paints and a sponge. For good measure, add "ancient" petroglyphs that appear to be worn by time and weather. This project introduces sponge painting with acrylic paints, a technique you'll use often.

Materials

- gourd, cleaned
- acrylic paints in earth tones, with accent colors
- flat black enamel spray paint
- clear matte spray finish
- white glue
- scrap leather
- artificial sinew or other lacing material
- antler slices or beads

Tools

- small handsaw or mini-jigsaw
- artist's sea sponge
- small paintbrush
- glover's needle
- awl

CUTTING, CLEANING, AND PREPARING THE GOURD

1 Cut the gourd open using a mini-jigsaw or handsaw. An uneven or slightly wavy opening lends to the rustic appearance of the piece, so don't worry if your cut is not perfect.

2 Clean the interior of the gourd thoroughly. Remove all residue of the gourd pulp lining the shell because any residue will show up differently under paints or dyes.

3 Spray the interior of the gourd with flat black enamel paint or leave it plain, as you prefer. For a different appearance, color the inside of the gourd with leather dyes or watered-down acrylic paints.

> **TIP:** A student in one of my classes complained that she ruined her gourd every time she tried to paint the interior. Upon further questioning, I learned that she was attempting to spray paint the inside of the gourd after completing all the exterior decoration. It is important to plan ahead and do each step in a logical sequence.

No matter which coloring agent you choose, be sure to finish the interior completely before investing a lot of time decorating the gourd exterior. To coat the interior with spray paint, hold the spray nozzle close to the gourd opening and carefully rotate the gourd until all interior areas are well covered.

Caution: For your health and safety, wear a vapor-rated respirator when working with sprays and aerosols.

The interior of the gourd is sprayed with flat black paint. Hold the can fairly close to the opening and rotate the gourd as you spray.

SPONGE PAINTING

4 Prepare a surface for use as a palette. While you might wish to purchase a commercial product, scrap paper with at least one unprinted side works great and is environmentally responsible. Fold the paper so the printing is on the inside; the double thickness of paper will hold up well. Puddle the paint directly onto the surface of the scrap paper, and use it to blot and mix your paints as you work. When you're finished with the project or you need a clean surface, merely throw the old sheet away and replace it with a fresh one.

Sponge painting looks best when you build multiple thin layers of color on the gourd surface. If you have a light touch, you can even paint so that some of the natural gourd surface coloration remains evident. Effective sponge painting takes a bit of practice, but don't worry about making mistakes; just continue to add layers of color until you are satisfied with the results. A sea sponge with small pores or openings will make a finer pattern and gradient of colors than you can get with a more open-textured sponge.

Choose three or four similar colors, but in different shades or tones. For example, a good choice for this project might be dark brown, reddish brown, tan, and cream. The actual colors aren't important; just try to choose some similar to those found in natural stone. Begin with the darkest color values and progress to lighter ones.

5 Squeeze a puddle of the darkest color onto the paper palette. Dampen the sponge completely by dipping it into a container of water and squeezing out as much excess water as possible. Dip the sponge in the puddle of paint, and blot any excess onto the adjacent clean area of the paper. Pat the sponge lightly over the entire gourd, allowing the gourd's natural color to show through the paint in some areas. Refresh the sponge with additional paint as needed.

Painting progression, showing the addition of each color layer. (Read across from left to right.)

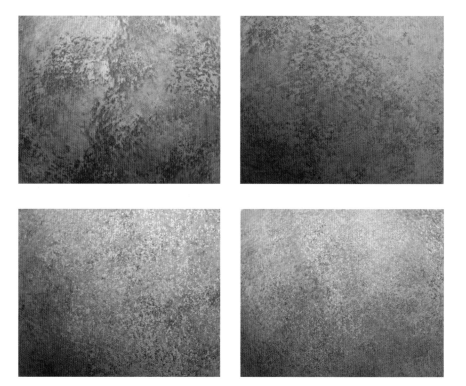

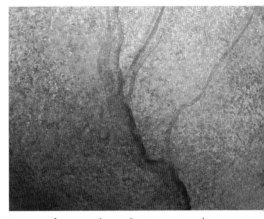

6 Build up successive layers of color from dark to light. Because sponging over a too-wet area will lift the previous layer and leave the underlying surface exposed, be sure to let each layer dry before adding another. With practice, you'll find that you can add subsequent layers of paint while the previous layer is just slightly damp. This will allow for a blending effect, producing subtle color variation.

7 Next, select one or two accent colors that will add just a hint of visual interest. I usually choose one metallic color, such as gold or copper, and one other for further interest. For this project, mossy green or a rusty red would be effective; both of these colors occur in the lichens and moss that grow on stones, and will add realism to the result. Apply the final colors sparingly. If you find they are too noticeable when you're done, lightly re-sponge those areas with some of your base color(s).

Painting faux cracks and striations on the rock surface.

8 Add some cracks and striations in the rock surface. Use a paintbrush and some colors of the darkest value to add irregular lines to various areas of the gourd; diagonal lines look pleasing to the eye. Don't make the lines too similar or straight. Look at a photo of a rock wall or a piece of marble or sandstone to get the idea.

9 Add the petroglyph designs as shown, or make up your own. Add a bit of water to the darkest-value paint to make it about half strength. Paint each small design with a brush and, just before the paint is completely dry, blot it with a clean, damp sponge to remove a small portion of the paint. This will make the petroglyph appear old and mottled. If you remove too much paint accidentally, repaint and re-blot until you like the effect.

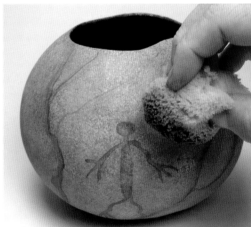

Paint petroglyph figures with a brush, then soften them with a sponge by removing a small amount of the wet paint.

10 Spray the finished painting with a sealer. Matte spray is ideal for simulating rocks.

Petroglyph Patterns

SIMPLE LACED-ON EMBELLISHMENTS

11 Use scrap leather for a decorative trim. Find it at leather crafting stores, some fabric stores, or cut it from a leather chamois made for car washing. Cut the strip so one side is reasonably straight and the other side is more uneven. Test fit the piece by laying it over the rim of the gourd and trim as necessary. Glue the leather strip to the gourd rim using just enough glue to hold the leather in place while the lacing is completed. A heavy-bodied white glue will work well and will not bleed through to stain the leather surface.

12 In preparation for lacing, use a sharp awl to make a series of holes around the rim of the gourd. The holes should pierce both the leather and the rim of the gourd, and they should be about ½ to 1 inch (12 to 25 mm) apart. Thread the sinew or other lacing material with a glover's needle. Glover's needles have a triangular, knife-like tip that easily pierces the leather if the awl doesn't produce a large enough hole.

Sew the leather on the gourd through the pre-punched holes. If necessary, use pliers to assist in drawing the lacing through the leather. When completed, tie a sturdy knot and leave long tails on the lacing.

13 Add an antler button or other large flat bead as a decorative accent. Thread the button onto the tails left from the lacing process. Tie it securely, and add beads to the ends, if desired.

VARIATION

Sponge painting is effective for simulating other surfaces. To create an aged patina effect, begin with a base coat of dark black/green paint. The second coat can be shades of mossy or turquoise green. Finish with a metallic accent color. Be sure to leave some of the previous colors exposed as you add new layers of paint.

Glue a strip of leather trim around the opening.

Punch holes through the leather and the gourd surface; then sew with sinew using a simple overhand stitch.

GOURD BUG PINS

Create a swarm of bug pins from small gourd scraps, and you'll get the itch that comes from the bite of the "gourd bug." Make your bugs as realistic or fantastic as you can imagine. Mix and match bodies and wings, and add bright colors, artful designs, and other embellishments. Every bug you make will be different, and soon your friends will be "bugging" you for pins of their own.

Materials

- gourd scraps, cleaned
- wood glue
- glue-on pin backings
- craft wire, various colors
- black fine-point permanent marker
- clear spray sealer (matte, semigloss, or gloss)
- acrylic paints or other coloring agents
- epoxy glue or gap-filling cyanoacrylate glue

Optional Materials

- beads and embellishments
- metallic leafing supplies
- rubber-stamping supplies

Tools

- small handsaw or mini-jigsaw
- hobby knife
- sandpaper
- wire cutters
- small drill bit and drill or pin vise
- spring-type clothespins or other small clamps
- small paintbrush
- wood burner (optional)

1 Make templates by copying and cutting the bug patterns from cardstock (see patterns on page 58). After you've made a few bugs, you may want to try changing the templates a bit to create other shapes. Trace the patterns onto gourd scraps, selecting scraps that are solid and reasonably flat. Save the thickest scraps for the bug bodies; thinner scraps are ideal for wings. Pairs of wings must be mirror images; flip the pattern over to draw the second wing. Try to match gourd scraps so pairs of wings will be similar in thickness and color.

2 Cut all the parts, and sand the edges and backs of each one. Make sure the back of the bug body has a flat area in the center where you can attach a pin back. Sand the wing pieces so they fit neatly against the curve of the body. When constructing multiple bugs, test fit sets of wings and bodies, and then tape the sets together or number the backs of each part in a set so you can identify them easily at any time.

3 Glue the wings onto the body, using a thin coat of wood glue. Clamp the parts together, and put the bug aside until the glue has set. In some cases, depending on the materials you choose, it may be easier to attach the wings after you decorate the bug.

TIP: Spring-type wooden clothespins make wonderful small clamps, or try removing the plastic pinch grips or metal spring clips from skirt or pant hangers.

Glue the bug bodies and wings, and clamp them in place. Keep sets together by taping them or marking the pieces with numbers.

Bug Patterns

ADDING EMBELLISHMENTS

4 Paint or decorate the bugs however you like, with acrylic paints or rubber-stamping products, such as embossing powders, stamps, or dye inks. You may want to try metallic leafing or specialty paints for interesting effects. Small jewelry-size projects such as this one are the best for experimenting with new materials. If you don't like the finished piece, at least you won't have ruined a large gourd.

5 These bugs are imaginary creatures, so go wild! Spiraled antennae or beaded legs will give your bugs greater interest. Make appendages from colored craft wire or jewelry head pins; string small beads onto the wires for a different look. (Jewelry head pins look like very long straight pins. Usually available in gold or silver, the pins are made from a flexible wire and are ideal for stringing beads.) Drill tiny holes where you want to attach the appendages, then place a dab of epoxy or gap-filling cyanoacrylate glue on the tip of the wire before pushing it into the predrilled hole. If the bug body is too thin to drill, glue the wire onto the backside of the pin.

6 Use epoxy glue to attach a pin backing to the back of the gourd bug. Be sure not to get any excess glue on the working parts of the pin.

GOURD DRUM NECKLACE

Despite its size, construction of this miniature gourd drum is similar to that of its full-size counterpart. Assembled from thin goatskin rawhide and a jewelry-size gourd, the finished drum makes a beautiful ornament or necklace. This is a simple project that is finished with no trouble in a few hours and is suitable for children.

Materials

- jewelry-size gourd, cleaned
- thin goatskin rawhide
- 4-ply waxed linen cord (any color)
- decorative beads
- white glue
- clear spray sealer

Tools

- pencil
- paper
- compass
- small handsaw or mini-jigsaw
- small scissors
- awl
- large sewing needle
- small rubber band

SELECTING, CLEANING, AND PREPARING THE GOURD

1 Select a mini gourd of any shape. A bottle-shaped gourd or one with a small neck is attractive and easy to use, but you can use any shape. In most cases, you'll turn the gourd upside down and cut the main opening from the bottom (or blossom) end. Mark the cutting line about one quarter of the way up from the bottom. On many full-size drums, the other end of the gourd is also removed to enable better resonation. This is optional, depending on the look you want to achieve. Cut the gourd along the marked lines and remove the pulp and seeds.

Cutting a section from the top of a small jewelry-size gourd. Save the small piece for future projects.

2 Sand the opening so the cut edge is completely flat and level. The easiest way to do this is to place the cut edge down on a piece of sandpaper and rotate the gourd until all edges are even and flat.

3 Paint, wood burn, dye, or decorate the shell, as you desire. Keep in mind that the top section of the gourd will be obscured by the upper edge of the drum skin and the lacing.

4 Spray the decorated shell with clear sealer.

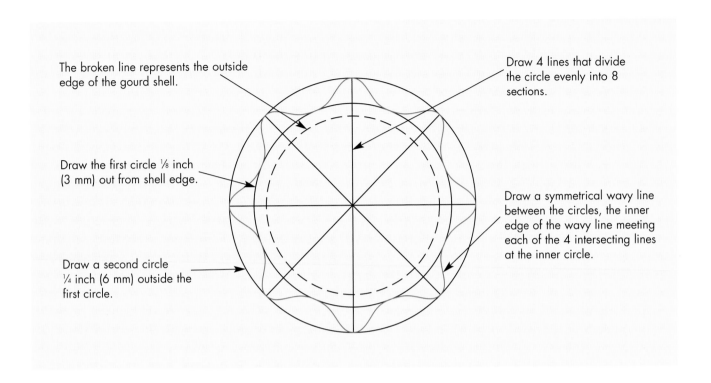

The broken line represents the outside edge of the gourd shell.

Draw 4 lines that divide the circle evenly into 8 sections.

Draw the first circle ⅛ inch (3 mm) out from shell edge.

Draw a symmetrical wavy line between the circles, the inner edge of the wavy line meeting each of the 4 intersecting lines at the inner circle.

Draw a second circle ¼ inch (6 mm) outside the first circle.

ASSEMBLING THE DRUM

5 Draw a paper pattern before cutting the leather drumhead. Use a compass to draw a circle that is slightly larger than the cut opening of the gourd (see the diagram above). When the gourd is centered inside the circle, the circle should extend about ⅛ inch (approximately 3 to 4 mm) beyond the gourd. Draw a second circle ¼ inch (approximately 6 mm) outside the first. Draw 4 lines through the circle that evenly divide it into 8 pie-shaped sections. In the space between the circles, draw a symmetrical wavy line that touches both circles; make the wavy line touch the inner circle 8 times, where it intersects each of the 4 lines you drew through the circle. When finished, the pattern will resemble a flower or sunburst in shape. Cut the pattern along this wavy line.

6 Select a piece of thin rawhide for the drum skin. Much thinner than cow rawhide, goatskin rawhide is a better choice for this project; it will lie more smoothly, making the finished drum look nicer. If you have a scrap left from a full-size drum project, see if you can cut a jewelry-size drumhead from it. Trace the pattern onto the rawhide and carefully cut the skin into the finished shape with small scissors. Use an awl or large sewing needle to poke

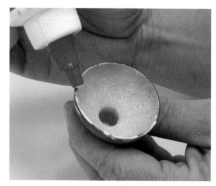

When you are finished decorating the gourd, add the drumhead. Place a small amount of glue around the top edge of the gourd.

Place the wet drumhead over the gourd and hold it in place with rubber bands.

Lace the drumhead onto the gourd, running the lacing back and forth from the drumhead to the cord around the gourd's neck.

a small hole in the center of each wavy projection, and then soften the skin by dipping the rawhide into room-temperature water. You don't need to soak the skin for very long; it will soften and become pliable quickly.

7 Rub a small amount of white glue on the cut edge of the gourd. Center the drumhead over the opening and bend the wavy projections over the sides. Use a small rubber band to hold the skin in place, and make minor adjustments until the skin looks smooth and even.

8 Lace the drum with a 3-foot (1-m) length of waxed linen cord. Tie a knot at one end of the cord, creating a loop that will fit snugly around the neck or bottom third of the gourd. This loop should have a 3- to 4-inch (7- to 10-cm) tail on one end; thread a needle onto the remaining long "working" end.

Place this cord loop around the neck or base of the gourd (see photo at bottom left on this page). Take the needle on the working end of the cord up to the first wavy projection on the drumhead and run it through the pre-punched hole. Pull the cord snug and then run it back down under the cord circling the neck. Continue threading back and forth through each wavy projection on the drumhead and under the loop of cord around the gourd's neck. When you get back to where you began, gently pull the cord snug to even the tension all around the drum. Be careful not to pull too hard or you may rip the drumhead. Tie the working end of the cord securely to the short tail of cord where you began. Trim the end of the cord, leaving a 3- to 4-inch tail. The drumhead will shrink and tighten as it dries.

9 Attach cord(s) to the drum for hanging. If you want to use the drum as an ornament, make a hanger from a small loop of waxed linen cord. To create a necklace, cut two pieces of cord 2 feet (60 cm) long. Use a needle to slip one end of a cord under one of the wavy drumhead projections. Tie a knot around the tensioning cords just under the skin, leaving one long end and a short tail. Repeat on the other side of the drum with the second piece of cord.

10 You may want to add decorative beads to the necklace cord. Choose beads that coordinate with the drum and select matching sets of beads for each side. Tie a stop knot in the necklace cord about 1 to 2 inches (2.5 to 5 cm) above the drum. Add a set of beads and tie another knot to hold them in place. Repeat on the opposite side of the drum. Tie the two loose ends of cord together at the desired necklace length, or make an adjustable sliding fastening.

CREATING AN ADJUSTABLE NECKLACE CORD

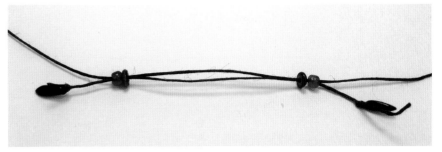

Make the necklace cord adjustable by threading the cords through a series of beads.

11 To make an adjustable fastening, choose either two or four beads with holes just large enough to allow two thicknesses of cord to pass through (see photo at top right). String all of the beads onto the end of one cord, and then run the other cord through the same beads from the opposite side. The loose tails will protrude from opposite ends of the row of beads. Tie an additional bead to the end of each loose tail. Grasp the sets of beads and pull them in opposite directions to shorten the necklace or pull the lower cords apart to lengthen it.

12 Add coordinating beads to decorate any remaining small cord tails. Tie a knot to hold the beads in place, and trim away any excess cord.

Beads accent the dangling cords.

GOURD MASKS

Different cultures the world over craft functional and artistic masks using wood, cloth, leather, feathers, and bone. Their shapes and other natural characteristics make gourds the perfect medium for creating modern-day art masks.

With some simple construction ideas and a handful of embellishments, you can turn out beautiful gourd masks. Learn the basic techniques of mask construction, and then let your creativity loose.

Materials

- gourd of any shape or size, cleaned
- coloring agent (dyes, paints, or inks)
- flat black spray paint
- clear spray sealer (matte or semigloss)
- thin leather cord or other sturdy hanging cord

Optional Materials

Be adventurous; you can use virtually anything, including these items.

- horsehair or feathers
- raffia or other grasses and reeds
- leather, fur, cloth, or other natural and woven fibers
- sinew
- beads
- stone or glass cabochons
- metallic cones or bells
- shells
- conchos (decorative pieces used on leather)
- porcupine quills, antler, bone, or horn
- seed pods
- wire

Tools

- pencil
- small handsaw or mini-jigsaw
- rotary tool and ball-shaped bur
- drill and drill bits
- sandpaper
- paint brushes or other color applicators

SELECTING, CLEANING, AND PREPARING THE GOURD

1 Select a gourd of any shape or size; even one with a flaw or a damaged side can be perfect for a mask. Long, thin gourds are especially appropriate for African styles, while round gourds are often used for Southwest styles.

2 Cut the gourd either lengthwise or crosswise. Cut the gourd in half to make two masks or remove only the back third for a more dimensional mask. A mask made from a whole gourd is very effective when displayed on a stand. Clean the gourd interior thoroughly, and sand the cut edges smooth and even, so the mask will lie flat against the wall. Spray the gourd interior with flat black paint.

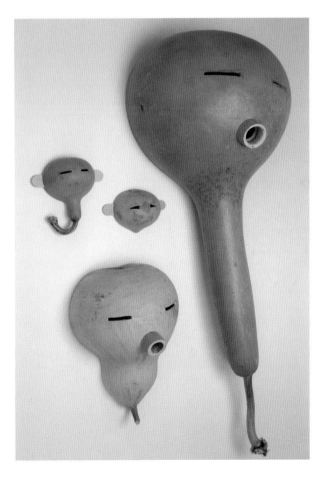

Gourds make masks of all shapes and sizes.

Patterns for Gourd Masks

CREATING THE MASK

3 Use a pencil to sketch some basic design elements on the gourd. It's easy to remove these marks later with a damp rag or baby wipe, so feel free to work on it until you're satisfied with the overall design.

Keep in mind that the eyes should be level across the gourd, unless you have a specific artistic reason for placing them otherwise. For nonfunctional masks, arrange the design elements any way you like. If you plan for the mask to be worn, put the eyeholes at an appropriate level for the wearer's comfort.

4 Add structural elements such as ears or mouth rings before you decorate the mask. A reflection of Navajo Yei and Pueblo Kachina designs, Southwest-style masks often feature mouth rings. Create a mouth ring by cutting a short length from a scrap gourd neck and gluing it to the front of the mask.

5 Cut the eyeholes with a small saw, and sand the opening smooth. If you intend to put glass globs, beads, or stones into the openings to embellish the eyes, be sure to cut the eyeholes an appropriate size.

6 You might want to pyroengrave decorative designs on the gourd shell. Complete the burning before you apply colors, because burning through paints or dyes can release toxic fumes. The burned lines will help if you plan to use thin pigments such as dyes or inks. The burned margins can separate colored areas and prevent mixing colors inadvertently.

7 Color the mask with your choice of coloring agent. Acrylic paints are the most colorfast, but dyes and inks produce a more transparent finish.

Choose the colors and media most appropriate for the style of your mask. Northwest Coast masks incorporate natural finishes or a limited palette of bold, painted colors. African masks usually feature dark, earthy colors, while shiny, lacquered colors and metallic paints or leafing often embellish Asian masks. Brightly painted colors characterize Southwest masks, but muted colors and decorative embellishments can also achieve a southwestern feel.

8 Seal the mask with a clear spray before adding embellishments.

Draw your design on the gourd after it's cut and cleaned. Cut out openings for the eyes and mouth.

The mask, after burning, coloring, and decorative carving.

Make a hanger by drilling holes through the top of the mask and adding a loop of leather or cord.

9 For added decorative effect, carve small dots or lines, using a rotary tool and a small ball-shaped bur. Carve the lines directly through the applied layer of color to add contrast and dimension. When the carving is complete, spray the mask with an additional layer of clear sealer.

10 Use a drill with a small bit to make two holes a short distance apart at the very top of the mask. Insert a short length of leather cord or other sturdy material into one of the holes and tie overhand knots both above and below the hole. Leave enough cord length to make a hanging loop and make a second pair of knots at the second hole. Neatly trim any excess cord.

ADDING EMBELLISHMENTS

11 Gather embellishment materials suitable to the style of your mask. Add a beard or hair of soft materials, and earrings or other decorations of hard materials; experiment with a variety for a distinctive appearance. Apply the ornamentation with the appropriate technique or adhesive.

Attach clumps of fibers, yarns, and raffia securely by threading them through pairs of holes drilled near the gourd's edges, or sew them directly onto the gourd through small holes drilled in the gourd shell.

Choose appropriate embellishments to accent the mask style. Consider using jute, raffia, horsehair, twine, pine needles, fibers, beads, metal cones, or porcupine quills.

Make horsehair bundles by wrapping sinew or thread around the end of a small bunch of hair. Trim the bundle directly below the sinew or thread, and coat the cut end with white glue. Insert the horsehair bundle directly into a hole drilled into the gourd shell, or glue it into large beads or metal cones for an extra decorative touch.

There are two ways to apply feathers with a neat finished appearance. The first is to drill holes into the gourd and individually insert the quill of each feather. This works well for large feathers or those that are to be widely spaced around the gourd.

The second method is to insert the feathers in air-dry clay. This method allows greater flexibility in placement and working time for adjustments, which is especially useful when applying a lot of feathers or feathers that are small. Some brands of air-dry clay come in colors that will blend with the mask and be less visible through any gaps in the feathers.

If you're using air-dry clay, apply a thin film of white glue to the gourd shell before adding the clay. Apply a layer of air-dry clay to the mask surface where you intend to place the feathers. The clay should be thick enough to hold several layers of feathers: the more feathers to be added, the heavier the layer of clay. Dip each feather into a bit of white glue before inserting it into the clay. Build layers of feathers in a pleasing pattern until you cover the clay. When the clay sets and hardens in a few hours, the feathers will be very secure.

You can glue leather, fur, and cloth directly to the gourd. Use thick-bodied white glue; unlike some other adhesives, this glue will not bleed through to create a visible stain.

Attach embellishments such as beads by drilling holes in the gourd shell, and use wire, jewelry head or eye pins, or cord or thread to secure the beads in place. Whenever possible, sew or use some sort of fastener to attach embellishments firmly to the gourd shell. Items that are merely glued on may eventually fall off.

Affix beads or cabochons for eyes with epoxy or other strong glue. A tight fit will assure that the bond remains secure.

Add raffia or yarn by drilling holes through the mask, and lacing the material through the holes. Knot the fibers on the outside of the mask.

Bundle the horsehair and wrap it with sinew or thread. Coat the wrapped end with glue, and insert the bundle into cones or beads, or directly into holes drilled into the mask.

NESTED VASES AND BOWLS

This simple but elegant project is a perfect way to rescue cut-off sections and tops from the gourd scrap pile. The smaller bowls rest inside the larger one, so they can have flat or rounded bases. The bottom half of a large gourd makes the biggest bowl, and it gives you a fine chance to redeem a flawed or cracked gourd. This southwestern example uses traditional Pueblo designs, but feel free to choose any theme or color combination.

Materials

- medium to large gourd half, cleaned
- assortment of small gourds or cut-off gourd tops
- acrylic paints
- clear protective sealer (matte or satin)

Tools

- pencil
- small handsaw or mini-jigsaw
- sandpaper or files
- paintbrush
- artist's sponge

CUTTING, CLEANING, AND PREPARING THE GOURDS

1 For the main bowl, select a gourd large enough to hold at least five to seven smaller ones. Cut the gourd, and sand or file the cut edge until it is smooth and level. Clean the gourd interior thoroughly, using sandpaper to smooth and remove any ridges or protrusions. You may have to modify the gourd's base to make it sit solidly; sand the high areas or use air-dry clay to build up low areas to make the bowl sit level.

2 Cut the small gourds or gourd parts as necessary to produce attractive vase or bowl shapes. Clean the interiors and finish the top edges. If using a cut-off gourd top, remove any remaining stem with pliers and smooth the area as much as possible. If you like, sand the bases of the small vessels flat so they can sit independently. A belt sander is the fastest and easiest way to do this, but be careful not to sand too far and create a hole in the bottom.

Small bowls can be cut from scrap pieces of almost any size and shape.

PAINTING AND DECORATING THE GOURDS

3 Determine what style you want to use on the grouping, and use the same design theme on all the vessels. Be sure that all the individual parts share some characteristic feature that unifies the project. For example, paint the pieces in a variety of related designs, all in the same colors, as in the photo at right. Similarly, you might use different colors in an otherwise consistent design theme.

One other technique to unify the grouping is to decorate the bowls in a set of related colors or tones; look at sample paint chips for good examples. You can create interest by employing a variety of shapes and textures, bearing in mind that the group is a distinct unit; make the individual parts blend with or complement each other.

4 Paint or decorate the bowls with materials appropriate to the style you have chosen. The examples shown here were sponge painted with several thin layers of acrylic in shades of rust, orange, and tan. They represent prehistoric and contemporary Pueblo symbols.

5 Spray or brush the pieces with a clear matte or satin protective sealer. When the pieces are dry, make a pleasing arrangement of them within the largest bowl.

After the small bowls are cut, cleaned, and sanded, paint them in a variety of native or other designs.

GOURD RISTRA

A Mexican tradition, the ristra *(pronounced rē-strӑ, meaning "string") is typically a string of chili peppers or garlic. In the Southwest, fresh ristras often hang in the kitchen, ready for use in cooking, or by the front door, as a familiar welcome sign.*

It's easy to make a gourd ristra, and it's an unusual accent that works both indoors and out. This ristra isn't edible, but it makes a wonderful gift that will last a long time.

Materials

- 10 to 15 mini-size gourds (hardshell or ornamental), cleaned
- raffia
- coloring agent (dyes, stains, or paint)
- clear UV-protective sealer for outdoor use
- baling or heavy craft wire for hanger

Tools

- drill with a $\frac{1}{16}$-inch (1.6-mm) drill bit
- scissors
- wire cutters
- dye applicator or paint brush
- disposable gloves

CUTTING, CLEANING, AND PREPARING THE GOURDS

1 Select a set of small gourds. The number needed will depend on the ristra's overall length and the size of the gourds. Pick whatever sizes and shapes you like, in keeping with availability and personal taste. Ornamental and hardshell varieties are equally practical.

2 Through the top of each gourd just below the stem, make a pair of stringing holes; with a small drill bit, pierce one side and pass at an even level to the other side of the gourd. Place this hole no more than about ½ inch (10 to 12 mm) below the stem.

3 Thread a small piece of craft wire through each gourd, and twist each wire into a loop. This serves as a little handle when applying color, and a temporary hanger while the gourd dries. Remove the wire prior to assembling the ristra.

> **TIP:** The gourds are more attractive when each has a stem, and it's easy to replace those that are missing or broken. First, remove any remnant of the old stem by grinding or sanding to smooth the stem attachment area. Cut or sand the base of the broken or replacement stem to assure it will sit securely in the gourd. Drill a small hole in the base of the stem and a corresponding hole in the gourd. Place a short length of dowel or round wooden toothpick into the hole in the stem; then insert the doweled stem into the hole in the gourd. Securely attach all the parts with wood glue.

Drill a hole through the top of each gourd.

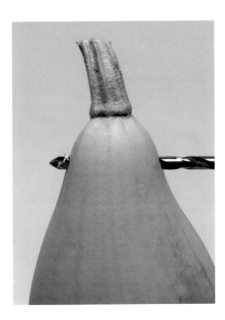

Repair a broken stem or replace one that's missing by adding a small dowel to the stem. Glue the dowel into the gourd.

USING OUTDOOR-SAFE COLORS AND FINISHES

4 Leave the gourds in their natural color, or use dyes, stains, paints, or even shoe polish to color them. Each medium has its advantages and disadvantages.

Leather dyes provide a lovely, somewhat transparent color, but fade rapidly when exposed to sunlight. Use leather dyes only if fading is acceptable or the item will hang indoors.

Rubber-stamping dye inks are a better choice for outdoor use. While these will also fade over time, the fading is usually less. Use a brand that is solvent based for best results and longer lasting color.

Acrylic and spray paints are more opaque, but provide the most lasting color and greatest durability.

5 Whatever coloring agent you choose, be sure to seal each gourd before assembling the ristra. Spray or brush on a weather-resistant, ultraviolet-protective coating for outdoor use. Spar varnish is very durable for outdoor use, but tends to yellow over time.

USING RAFFIA TO ASSEMBLE THE RISTRA

6 String and decorate the ristra with raffia. Raffia frequently comes packaged in a tight bundle full of kinks and bends. Prepare the raffia by wetting the bundle thoroughly to relax the fibers, and hang the bundle to dry. The weight of the wet raffia will usually pull it straight, or you can smooth it with your fingers as it dries.

7 Thread one long, sturdy piece of raffia through a gourd. Occasionally, the raffia fibers will separate or split, making it difficult to draw the raffia through the holes. If necessary, thread the raffia through a large-eye needle or a long loop of wire first.

After the raffia is through the gourd, pull enough length to the other side to tie it into a double knot. Pull the knot tight so it lies snugly against the gourd.

Pull a second, shorter piece of raffia through the knotted strand and tie a decorative bow, like a shoestring. A double knot will hold the bow in place; apply a dab of white glue to hold it more securely. Do this for each gourd.

Apply dye, stain, or paint to each gourd.

Use a needle or a loop of wire to help draw the raffia through the stringing holes at the top of the gourd.

Tie the raffia ends in a knot at the top of the gourd.

Tie a bow around the stem.

It may be easier to arrange the gourds if they are first tied into bunches of three.

8 Gather the long ends of raffia from the gourds in one hand and adjust the grouping to the desired length with your other hand. Stagger the gourds down the length of the ristra; place the smaller ones near the top, the larger gourds toward the base, and add or remove them as necessary to create a flowing pattern. When you have the desired arrangement, numerous lengths of raffia will extend from your closed hand.

Gather another small bundle of raffia and add it to the material in your hand, arranging it behind the grouping, and letting it fall slightly beyond the bottom gourd.

Tie the entire gourd and raffia bundle together with an overhand knot, several inches above the topmost gourd. Make sure that all the strands are included within the knot. Then, gently pull each individual strand at both ends of the knot; this will tighten any loose strands and tighten the knot.

Trim away the excess raffia, cutting the strands evenly several inches above the knot. Fan out the loose ends decoratively (see photo on page 72).

9 Just below the large knot, tie an attractive raffia or fabric bow, whether a simple cross-loop (the kind used to tie shoestrings) or an elaborate florist's style. Think about adding conchos or hanging feathers.

10 Force a small piece of wire through the knot and the bow, and twist the wire ends together to create a hanging loop. Your ristra is ready to hang and enjoy.

A gathering of gourds, staggered in a flowing pattern.

GOURDS AND BOTANICALS WREATH

A handsome botanical wreath at your front door always makes visitors feel welcome, and the natural style of this example makes it perfect for indoor decorating. Make it entirely from mini gourds, or a mixture of gourds and local or purchased botanicals. Add an accent bow to coordinate with the season and enjoy your wreath year-round.

Materials

- mini gourds of any shape, cleaned
- thick foam ring or straw wreath
- Spanish moss
- construction adhesive
- spray adhesive
- clear spray sealer (matte or semigloss)
- floral picks or bamboo skewers
- sturdy wire

Optional Materials

- ¹⁄₁₆-inch (1.6-mm) plywood or stiff cardboard
- pods, nuts, or dried fruit
- ribbon or raffia, for a bow

Tools

- pencil
- newspaper
- small jigsaw or sharp craft knife
- caulking gun
- drill and small drill bit

PREPARING THE WREATH BASE

1 Buy a thick foam ring or cut one from a large piece of hard foam. If you use a straw wreath for the base, it will be much more difficult to insert the botanicals. The finished wreath will be a good deal wider than the base, so plan accordingly.

Create a sturdy wire hanger for the wreath. Wrap a length of wire once or twice around the foam ring, and twist the wire ends together at the back. Use the excess wire to fashion a small loop for hanging. Securely twist the remaining wire ends together, then trim and push the excess wire into the foam.

The wreath begins with a foam ring, an optional backing board, a caulking gun, and a tube of construction adhesive.

2 Add a backing to the base to protect the foam and give a finished appearance to the reverse side of the wreath. Cut the backing from a piece of thin plywood or heavy, non-corrugated cardboard. The thin plywood is sold at lumberyards as "door skins"; at woodworking or hobby stores, it's called aircraft grade or birch plywood. Heavy cardboard such as mat, foam core, or illustration board are acceptable substitutes, but use them only on wreaths to be displayed indoors.

Place the wreath on the backing material and trace around the inside and outside of the ring. Cut the backing material along this pattern.

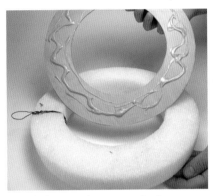

Attach the wire hanger to the foam ring. Then coat the backing board with construction adhesive and press it onto the back of the ring.

3 Glue the backing to the rear of the foam with construction adhesive. Available at most hardware and home improvement stores, construction adhesive is inexpensive and very durable, with a heavy consistency that makes it easy to apply without dripping; it's compatible with foam products and it has flexibility, providing at least ten minutes of working time. Unlike the hot melt glue used in glue guns, this adhesive provides a permanent bond that is nearly impervious to extreme heat and cold. You can find construction adhesive in small tubes, but for a large project like this, it's more economical to purchase a caulking gun cartridge. One cartridge is usually more than enough to finish a wreath.

4 Lay the foam wreath backside down on several sheets of newspaper, and coat the entire surface with spray adhesive. Place the wreath on a fresh layer of clean newspaper for the next step.

Spray the foam ring with adhesive, and apply a thin layer of Spanish moss.

Prepare small gourds by drilling holes in the back and gluing in floral picks.

5 Apply a thin layer of Spanish moss to the entire foam surface to cover the underlying material and disguise any gaps between the added botanicals and gourds. Press the moss firmly into the adhesive and remove any excess that does not adhere well. Save the excess and any small remaining bits for use later.

ASSEMBLING THE WREATH

6 Gather an assortment of gourds and a variety of other botanical materials to make attractive accents. Some botanicals you might find interesting and readily available are devil's claws; jacaranda, okra, poppy, or yucca pods; dried ornamental oranges or orange slices; sweet gum balls; walnuts; dried pomegranates; small pine cones; eucalyptus sprigs; palm spirals; and acorns. Find these materials and many others locally, or buy them from a craft store.

Choose gourds in small to mini sizes and assorted shapes. Gourds in their natural finish are very attractive, but if you want to dye or paint them, do so prior to assembling the wreath. Dyed gourds will fade over time when exposed to sunlight, but the softer look of the faded colors is no less appealing.

7 Drill a small hole in the back of each gourd and insert a short floral pick or length of bamboo skewer. Hold the pick in place with a small dab of adhesive, for added strength. Give any round botanical items, such as oranges and nuts, a stronger mounting by doing the same to them.

8 Arrange the gourds on the wreath. Move them around until you're satisfied with the overall arrangement, or if you're adventurous, attach them permanently as you work. Place a blob of adhesive around the pick and on the back of the gourd, and push the gourd firmly into the wreath backing.

If you want to cover the entire wreath with gourds, place them close together and fill any small gaps with moss. If you plan to mix gourds and botanicals, place small clusters of gourds first, then fill in around them with other materials. Fill any noticeable gaps with small items or bits of moss. Glue pods directly in place by putting a blob of adhesive on the stem end, and pushing the pod firmly into the foam base.

Make the back of the wreath as neat and finished as the front. Cover any visible excess adhesive with a bit of moss. Allow the completed wreath to dry overnight.

Apply a blob of construction adhesive to the back of the gourd, then press the floral pick and the gourd firmly into the wreath base. Add other large botanicals in the same manner.

Attach smaller pods by daubing some adhesive on one end and pressing the pod firmly into the foam.

Cover any excess adhesive on the back with small bits of moss.

9 Spray the completed wreath with clear sealer.

10 Create a bow from ribbon or raffia, and secure it by twisting a piece of wire around the center of the bow. Tie a floral pick into the wire, and push the pick into a gap on the wreath. Attaching the bow with a pick makes it easy to change; you can quickly update your wreath to coordinate with the season.

VARIATION

This wreath relies chiefly on other botanicals, and features only a small number of gourds.

BARREL CACTUS BIRDFEEDER

Birds will flock to enjoy seeds and treats from this decorative barrel cactus birdfeeder. Cut from a large gourd, three wide openings provide plenty of room to accommodate multiple feathered friends. The feeder's rounded shape and single hanging cord make it unstable and less attractive to invading squirrels.

Materials

- large bushel basket or basketball gourd, cleaned
- one or more scrap gourd tops
- acrylic paints (various shades of green, plus yellow, red, gray, and white)
- ¹⁄₁₆-inch (1.6-mm) steel cable or braided wire and crimps, or heavy cord for hanging
- exterior-rated wood glue
- short piece of ¼-inch (6-mm) dowel
- exterior-rated sealer (polyurethane or spar varnish)

Tools

- pencil
- length of string or masking tape
- small handsaw or mini-jigsaw
- hand file or sandpaper
- compass
- drill with ¼-inch and ⅛-inch (6-mm and 3-mm) drill bits
- artist's sea sponge
- paint brushes (long liner and flat)
- wire cutters
- pliers

CUTTING AND CLEANING THE GOURD

1 Select a large round gourd that is reasonably thick, so it will be able to withstand both the weight of the feed and several birds.

TIP: While the project shown here uses a barrel cactus, you can make the same style feeder from bottle, kettle, or other large gourds.

2 Draw a line around the circumference of the gourd, about a third of the way up from the bottom. This line marks the base of the feeder openings. Make sure this line high enough to allow sufficient depth for a good quantity of seed.

Divide the gourd's circumference into equal thirds, placing three small marks on the line you just penciled. Measure the distance between the marks to confirm they are evenly spaced; do this by placing a length of string or masking tape from one mark to the next. Remove the strip and compare it to the distances between the other pairs of marks. Make any necessary adjustments before proceeding.

With a compass, draw three large semicircles on the gourd, using the three marks you just made as the centering points. These arcs define the top of the feeder openings. Leave several inches between each arc to maintain the gourd shell's strength. Round the corners slightly where the half circles meet the base line: this affords additional strength and reduces the possibility of future stress cracks.

Cut three symmetrical openings in the gourd, allowing enough depth in the bottom to hold plenty of birdseed.

3 Cut the three openings with a small handsaw or mini-saw. Make a small slit with a hobby knife to begin each cut, or drill a small hole. Save the cutout pieces for future projects. Clean the gourd thoroughly, and smooth any rough edges that remain by filing or sanding. Make a few holes in the very bottom of the feeder with a drill and a small drill bit to keep water from standing in the feeder after a rain.

4 Decorate the top of the feeder with one or more gourd "flowers." This is a wonderful way to use scrap gourd tops from other projects. Real barrel cactus flowers have narrow, multi-layered petals with pointed ends; simple gourd flowers with five or more rounded petals will do nicely here.

Cut small flowers from scrap gourd tops. Add dowels to the bottom of each flower.

Draw a scalloped line around each gourd top, creating a flower-like design. Cut along the scalloped line, and use a file or sandpaper to smooth the edges of each flower petal.

Attach each flower to the top of the feeder with a doweled joint. In most cases, attach the flowers so they point directly out from the feeder. Cut off any remaining stem, and flatten the base of the flower with a file or sandpaper. Drill a ¼-inch (6-mm) hole into the base of the flower where the stem was removed, and glue in a short length of wooden dowel.

Decide where to attach the flowers to the feeder, and drill a hole for each. Trim the dowels to make them flush with the gourd's interior. Wait until all the painting is done to glue the flowers in place.

Drill a tiny hole near the base of each flower to keep rainwater from collecting inside. For good drainage, place this hole at the lowest point on the flower.

Drill holes into the top of the feeder where you intend to place the flowers. Glue the flowers into the top after all the painting is complete.

PAINTING FOR EFFECT

TIP: For the birds' safety, leave the feeder's interior unpainted. If you must use a sealer, choose one rated to be nontoxic when dry.

5 Most barrel cactus flowers are yellow, orange, or reddish in color. Using a sponge, paint the flowers with layers of different shades to make them appear more dimensional. Highlight the tips of the petals, and deepen the color at the base and center of each flower. Use a small paintbrush to add details, such as the margins between the petals and a dark vein running down the center of each petal.

6 The barrel cactus has prominent ribs, giving it a pleated, accordion-like appearance. The actual cacti are giant water reservoirs, swelling and expanding with the rainfall, and shrinking inward during periods of drought. To create this pleated effect, paint the cactus so it appears lightest where the ribs bulge out and darker in the folds between the ribs.

Begin by sponge painting the entire birdfeeder with a base coat of medium sage or grayish green. Add a tiny bit of yellow to the paint and lightly apply another layer, allowing some of the background layer to show through. This gives the base coat a softer, less flat appearance.

Add a series of vertical stripes around the cactus, using a slightly deeper shade of green paint and a small artist's sea sponge. Don't make the edges of the stripes sharp and even. Instead, blend them slightly into the adjacent lighter-colored stripe. Paint the stripes narrowest at the top and bottom, expanding around the belly of the gourd. Stagger their placement; alternating them with stripes of the underlying background color.

Apply an additional layer of the darker green with a sponge, deepening the color down the center of each dark stripe. Finish with a flat brush and the darkest value green, creating a dark stripe down the center of the sponged area.

Add a bit of white paint to lighten the original sage green, and highlight the center of each lighter stripe with it. Apply the color with a small sponge and blend the edges so there are no hard lines. Add small blobs of light gray along this highlighted area, placing them a couple of inches (5 cm) apart. These will form the base for each bunch of needles.

Use a long liner brush to paint three or four dark green cactus needle shadows, angling the shadows downward from each of the needle base areas.

Apply base coat, using several different shades.

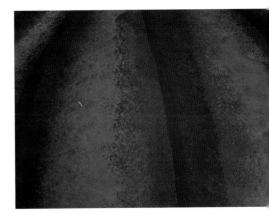

Add vertical striping with a sponge and brush.

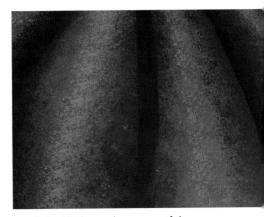

Apply highlights to the center of the stripes, using a sponge.

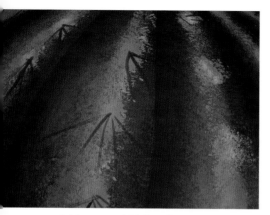

Add sponged blobs of paint where the cactus needles will be clumped. Add dark needle shadows with a liner brush.

A close-up view shows the detail in the finished painting. The needles were painted with a liner brush.

Glue on the flowers after the painting is finished, and add the hanging cable.

Finally, add some cactus needles. Paint the needles in a cream, tan, or even reddish color. Make the needles fan outward from a central base, and vary their length and thickness.

7 When the painting is finished, attach the gourd flowers by gluing them into the pre-drilled holes. Complete the gourd by spraying or brushing on an exterior-rated clear finish.

TIP: Add an interesting accent to the gourd flowers using fine copper wire. Drill a hole in the center of each flower, and glue in a small bundle of wire, creating "stamens."

HANGING AND SUPPORTING THE BIRDFEEDER

8 Fine steel braided cable, sometimes referred to as airplane control wire, is a strong hanging material that will not break or deteriorate in the weather. Hardware stores and hobby shops that cater to model airplane enthusiasts will usually stock it, and they sell it by the foot. Drill two small holes at the top of the gourd for the cable, placing the holes on opposite sides of the thick stem area. Make sure the gourd flowers will not interfere with the cable.

Use a small crimp to attach the cable or wire to the feeder. Crimps look like two connected parallel tubes. Run the wire through one side of the crimp, then into and back out of the feeder, and back into the other side of the crimp. Tighten the crimp by squeezing it with a pair of pliers or flattening it with a hammer. Use the same method to create a hanging loop on the other end of the wire, or to fasten the feeder over a tree branch. A shorter cable will lessen the risk of wind damage. Use other, more rigid hangers where strong winds are a concern.

Birds feel more secure when a tree shelters their feeder, but squirrels are apt to raid it from nearby branches. The feeder's spinning and swaying will deter them and most large birds, such as pigeons, jays, and doves.

Fill the feeder with sunflower or other seeds; then wait for the birds to discover their new dining area.

NATIVE RATTLE

Rattles are ancient percussive devices, used worldwide in vastly diverse cultures. One of mankind's oldest instruments, rattles have been made from animal hooves, turtle shells, rawhide, and pottery. Many cultures imbue rattles with magical or spiritual qualities, and children and adults alike find them irresistible. Gourds are a natural choice for making rattles; the example here is typical of those still used in Pueblo cultures.

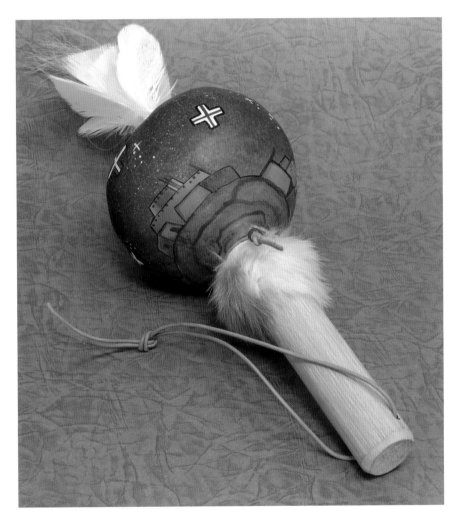

Materials

- softball-size gourd, cleaned
- wooden dowel pieces in 1-, ½-, and ⅛-inch (25-, 13-, and 3-mm) diameters
- seeds, beans, beads, rice, or other noisemakers
- acrylic paints (deep blue, white, red, brown, gold)
- fine-point permanent marker
- wood glue
- clear spray sealer (matte or gloss)
- newspaper sheets

Tools

- small handsaw or mini-jigsaw
- hand file and/or sandpaper
- drill with ½- and ⅛-inch (12- and 3-mm) drill bits (brad-point bits, if available)

An easy way to make a handle is to fit together different size dowels. Taper the end of the larger dowel to fit snugly into the opening in the gourd shell.

Test fit the handle to assure a tight fit in the gourd shell.

CUTTING AND CLEANING THE GOURD

1 Choose a small, softball-size gourd. Look for a small cannonball, canteen, or pear-shape gourd.

2 Cut two small holes on opposite ends of the gourd. Center these holes in most gourds at the blossom and stem ends. In canteen gourds, it's also attractive to run the handle through the gourd's width. Decide first which end of the gourd will be the base, the end with the handle. Cut this hole slightly less than 1 inch (25 mm) wide. The hole at the other end should be ½ inch (12 mm) wide.

> **TIP:** While it's possible to drill the holes in the gourd, this may chip or crack the shell. It's better to make the cuts with a small handsaw or mini-jigsaw. Smooth the cuts as needed with a round file or sandpaper wrapped around a dowel.

3 Remove the seeds and as much pulp as possible. Fill the gourd with gravel and shake it briskly to break up the remaining pulp. The cleaner the gourd interior, the better the rattle will sound. It isn't necessary here, but some cultures even boil the gourd shell to cleanse and harden it.

CREATING A HANDLE

4 The rattle's handle will pass completely through the gourd; this type of handle is very secure because it contacts the gourd shell in two places. Native artisans carve their handles to a taper, using local wood; here, two pieces of dowel make the handle.

Cut a section of the thickest dowel to the desired handle length, measuring from the base of the gourd shell. Cut a second piece at least 2 inches (5 cm) longer than the gourd's body from the mid-size dowel; you'll run this piece through the gourd, so it must extend well beyond the ends.

5 Make a small starter hole in the center of one end of the thickest dowel. Carefully drill a ½-inch- (12-mm-) diameter hole of sufficient depth to hold the smaller-diameter dowel firmly in place.

TIP: Prevent damage to the handle by wrapping the thick dowel in a protective layer of cloth or padding; then clamp it in a vise for stability during drilling. Use caution as you drill; the bit can easily slip. The safest is a brad-point drill bit; a small spike stops the bit from wobbling.

6 Glue the smaller dowel into the larger dowel, and set the pieces aside to dry. When the handle is solidly bonded, do a test fit: insert the handle's smaller end gently through the holes in the gourd, beginning with the base. The fit should be snug at both the top and bottom; trim the handle or the holes as necessary to achieve a good fit.

Native rattles typically have pegged handles, allowing the easy removal and replacement of a broken shell while preserving the handle. If you like, drill a ⅛-inch- (3-mm-) hole through the top of the handle immediately above the top of the gourd shell. Insert a short length of tapered ⅛-inch- (3-mm-) dowel in this hole to hold the shell in place without the need for glue.

You can secure the handle to the rattle without using glue: just force a short length of dowel through a hole drilled at the top of the handle.

DECORATING THE RATTLE

7 Remove the handle and decorate the gourd shell, as desired. Rattles from cultures native to the Southwest usually feature geometric patterns in bold colors. Use the designs suggested here or create your own.

TIP: Let your imagination run wild using other colorants or decorative styles. Try leather dye or paste wax for a beautiful natural finish, or experiment with pyroengraving or carving.

PAINTING THE RATTLE SHOWN

8 Apply a base coat of rich, deep blues, using acrylic paints. Apply the deepest tones at the top of the gourd with a sponge, and gradually lighten the color as you work toward the base.

Splatter "stars" across the blue sky. This can be messy, so cover the work area with sheets of newspaper or other disposable material. Find commercial splattering tools at art stores, or simply use a discarded toothbrush. Dampen the toothbrush slightly, and scrub the damp bristles into a bit of slightly

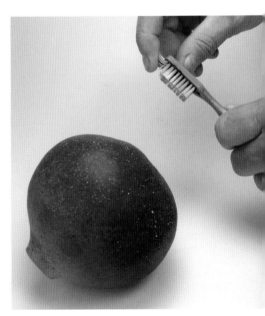

Paint the prepared gourd shell with a base coat and splatter it with "stars."

thinned, white acrylic paint. Hold the toothbrush 3 to 4 inches (7 to 10 cm) away from the area you want to paint, the bristles toward the gourd. Stroke your finger or an implement gently across the bristles, creating a spray of fine paint droplets. Learn to control the effect with practice; work out the distance you hold the brush from the gourd, the amount and thickness of the paint load, and the pressure you apply to the bristles.

Paint the mesa or pueblo designs around the gourd's bottom edge using two or more shades of brown or tan. With white acrylic, paint large, cross-shaped stars in the sky, a mixture of simple and complex stars of various sizes. Add a bit of color with touches of red or metallic gold paint. For greater detail, outline the designs with paint or a fine-point permanent marker.

Seal the finished gourd with a clear satin or matte spray when paints or dyes have dried. A waxed gourd requires no further finish.

Rattle Designs

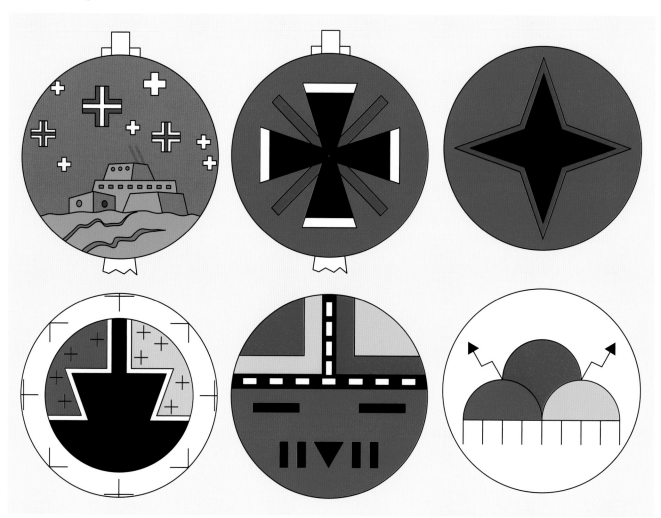

ASSEMBLING THE RATTLE

9 Fill the gourd shell with a handful of noisemaking material. The sound varies with the noisemaker; for instance, rice gives a soft, gentle swish, while glass beads produce a sound more sharp and bright. Native rattles commonly use corn and beans. Test different kinds and amounts of material until you find the sound you want.

10 Paint it, stain it, or leave the handle natural, and peg or glue it in place. Use only minimal glue to attach the handle. Smear a bit on the inside edge of each hole in the gourd and wipe off any excess when the handle is seated. Set the rattle aside to dry before applying further decorations.

11 Decorate the finished rattle with horsehair, leather, feathers, or whatever else pleases you. Tie, glue, or insert the items into holes drilled into the top of the handle. Exercise your imagination to decorate the lower portion with a leather thong, beads, or bells.

VARIATIONS

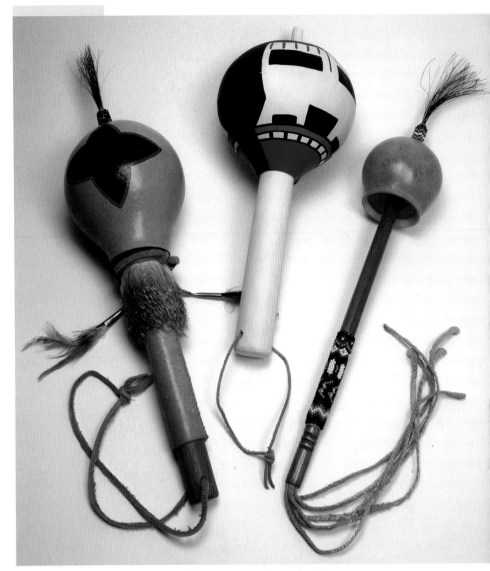

A trio of rattles, featuring various designs, materials, and techniques.

DRAGONFLY POTPOURRI OR CANDLEHOLDER

Practice your cutting skills to fashion a piece as functional as it is attractive. A glass candle cup hangs inside the gourd, where a burning tea light or votive safely glows. The flickering light creates a warm ambience and, through the decorative cutouts, it makes dragonfly shadows dance on the walls. A bit of potpourri at the bottom adds fragrance too, released by the candle's warmth.

Materials

- small gourd, cleaned
- glass bell-shape candle insert
- cardstock or other stiff paper
- flat black spray paint
- acrylic paints
- acrylic interference (iridescent) paints (blue and/or green)
- black fine-point permanent marker
- gold leafing supplies (optional)
- clear spray sealer (semigloss)

Tools

- compass
- small handsaw or mini-jigsaw
- small hand file
- hobby knife
- sandpaper
- small drill bit and drill or pin vise
- small paintbrush
- burning tool (optional)

TIP: Sold most often through craft stores or floral supply houses, glass bell inserts may be hard to find. If so, try to find another similar glass vessel or holder. Otherwise, make a smaller version of this project, using a flared glass votive holder, or just use the container for potpourri.

Cut a circular hole in the gourd so the bell-shape insert hangs from the rim and fits inside. Penciled lines indicate where the design will be.

CUTTING AND CLEANING THE GOURD

1 Choose a small, melon-size gourd—a cannonball, canteen, whatever shape you prefer. Be sure it's deep enough that the body of the glass insert will fit completely inside it. If necessary, file or sand the gourd's bottom so it sits flat. The gourd must be stable for safe candle burning.

2 Mark a circle on the top of the gourd using a compass; make it slightly smaller than the diameter of the glass insert. Before cutting, confirm that the circle is level and parallel to the base. Cut the gourd with a small saw and clean the interior thoroughly.

3 Test fit the glass insert, and enlarge the circular hole as necessary. Make minor adjustments with a hand file until the glass insert sits properly. Be sure that the flared edge of the insert rests firmly and evenly on the rim of the hole.

DESIGNING AND MAKING DECORATIVE CUTS WITH A MINI-SAW

The gourd now sports a dragonfly design. Place the grasses so they support the dragonfly wings. Draw an x or color in the areas you intend to cut out.

4 Draw two sets of level lines around the gourd. Draw the first line about an inch (25 mm) from the top of the gourd and the second about halfway down the gourd, creating a band approximately 2 inches (5 cm) wide. Add a second set of lines just outside (above and below) the first ones; these will be decorative borders for the design.

5 Copy the dragonfly pattern given on a piece of cardstock or other stiff paper. Cut out the pattern to create a template. Trace around the template in drawing the pattern for your gourd design, marking directly on the gourd. Scatter six or seven dragonflies between the bands. Here and there, let some small bits of the wings overlap other dragonflies or the decorative outer borders. Place a mark or color in each area you plan to cut out.

Drill small holes in each area to be removed; then cut out each section with a mini-saw.

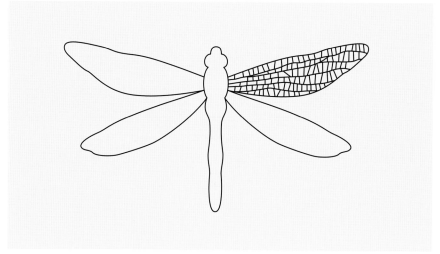

Trim any rough edges or corners with a sharp hobby blade.

Ensure the structural integrity of the cutout design. When you finish placing and spacing the dragonflies, add seemingly random blades of grass and a few small, simple flowers to tie the design together, secure it to the borders, and strengthen the cutout areas. Take a few minutes to examine your design; confirm that there are no fragile or inadequately attached dragonfly parts.

6 Use a rotary tool or pin vise with a small drill bit to pierce starter holes in each section to be removed. Place the saw tip into a drilled starter hole, and cut the sections slowly and carefully. Use care when rotating the saw to avoid breaking delicate parts.

TIP: When cutting a section that has tight corners, make multiple small cuts to avoid breakage. First, cut out the main area, using gently rounded curves; don't worry about cutting out the corners. Finish the corner by making two small cuts that approach the corner from opposite sides.

Clean up any rough edges and make fine adjustments with a small file or hobby knife, and give all the cut edges a final touchup with sandpaper.

Dragonfly Pattern

PAINTING AND FINISHING

7 After you complete the cutting and sanding, spray the gourd interior with flat black spray paint. Angle the spray to coat all the cut edges. Should any paint overspray flow through the holes and mark the outer shell, wipe it off with a paper towel and turpentine.

8 Use a burning tool to add clarity and dimensional effects to the finished design; burn the outer lines of the border and those areas where elements touch or overlap.

9 Leave the upper and lower sections of the gourd natural, or color them, if you like. The example here was lightly misted with a wood tone spray lacquer, covered more heavily toward the base.

10 Apply a thin wash of black acrylic paint to touch up any cut areas not fully covered by the black spray. The thin acrylic will soak in quickly; wipe any excess from the surface. If it seems a little tedious, this important step is the key to the finished project's professional appearance.

11 Paint the grass with shades of green acrylic paint, including areas that appear to pass behind the dragonfly wings. Paint the bodies of the dragonflies black, and add details around the eyes, thorax, and abdomen in blue or green. Paint the small flowers white, with a tiny yellow center.

12 Color the dragonfly wings with blue or green acrylic interference paint. Interference paint is a colorless, transparent medium containing titanium-coated mica flakes. These paints appear white in the bottle and translucent against white or light backgrounds. Darker backgrounds reveal their iridescent effect most intensely. The grass stems show through the interference paint, as if through dragonflies' shimmering, transparent wings.

13 Detail the wings with tiny veins, as in the pattern on page 92. Make the vein lines slightly irregular, as they are in nature. If you use a fine-point permanent marker, test it first to ensure it's compatible with the finish. Pen and ink is less likely to bleed or run when coated with a finish.

Paint the grasses first, extending the color across the dragonfly wings. Paint the wings later with translucent interference paints, which allow the grass to be visible through the wings.

Gourds and Candles Safety Tips

• Never leave a candle burning unattended.

• Gourds are extremely flammable. Do not use an open flame in a gourd without some type of protective glass container.

• Place candles out of the reach of children and pets.

• Extinguish the flame before the candle is fully consumed. Allowing the candle to burn away completely will place heat stress on the glass container, possibly causing it to fracture.

Add the candleholder. If you don't have a bell insert, substitute a small votive holder. Add potpourri to the base for a lovely fragrance.

14 Paint the upper and lower borders with a contrasting color, such as metallic gold or deep red, or try gold leaf as a pleasing complement to the iridescent dragonfly wings (see Ripples and Streams, page 123, for complete gold leafing instructions). Add a finish of several light applications of clear spray; multiple light applications are less likely to cause marker bleed than one heavy coat of spray.

TIP: For ease in cleanup, add a teaspoon of water or a thin layer of sand to the bottom of the glass container before adding the candle. The remaining wax will pop right out when the candle is extinguished and the remaining wax has hardened.

KIVA POTTERY

Step into the Southwest with this stylized Pueblo vase, featuring an abundance of surface treatment. Faux weaving, delicate miniature gourd pottery, and a pueblo ladder decorate its dimensional, stucco-like finish. The elaborate textural effect disguises major flaws in a raw gourd that might otherwise be unusable.

Materials

- gourd, cleaned
- scrap gourd neck (optional)
- flat black enamel spray paint
- air-dry clay
- acrylic paints (earth tones)
- sandstone paint (optional)
- small dowel pieces or round toothpicks
- wood glue
- clear spray sealer (matte or satin)

Tools

- pencil
- masking tape
- small handsaw or mini-jigsaw
- hand file and/or sandpaper
- artist's sea sponge
- small paintbrush
- drill and a $^{1}/_{16}$-inch (1.6-mm) bit

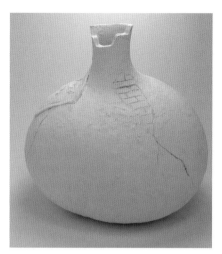

Coat the entire gourd with a thin layer of air-dry clay. Add the stucco-like texture and decorative features to the surface while it's wet.

CUTTING AND CLEANING THE GOURD

TIP: Though any gourd will do for this project, with a kettle- or bottle-shape one, you can skip the first step below. I chose to use a canteen gourd and a scrap gourd neck. The added neck increased the piece's height and made the shape more interesting. Having multiple surface flaws, this particular gourd wasn't suitable for most other projects.

1 Cut the ends of a scrap neck piece parallel, so it somewhat resembles a tube, but with at least one end slightly flared. Sand or file the wider flared end of the scrap, adding a slight inward bevel. Test fit the piece periodically until it sits solidly on the top of the gourd. Cut the other end with a decorative notch. Mark a cutting line on the gourd to ensure an opening smaller in diameter than the scrap neck and wide enough to provide a strong glue bond for the neck. Cut the opening with a mini-jigsaw or handsaw, and file or sand the edges as needed. Thoroughly clean the interior of the gourd, removing all gourd pulp residue.

2 Glue the neck on top of the gourd, hold it in place with masking tape, and set the gourd aside to let the glue cure.

3 Spray the interior of the gourd with flat black enamel spray, or whitewash it with diluted acrylic paint in the color you plan to use on the exterior.

SALVAGING A FLAWED GOURD

4 Apply a thin layer of air-dry (paper) clay to the entire surface of the gourd. This strengthens a thin-shelled gourd and disguises holes, seams, cracks, and flaws; it also gives an interesting texture. Mix a small amount of clay with a tablespoon or more of water in a shallow bowl or jar; blend it to the consistency of toothpaste. With wet fingers, spread the clay over the gourd's surface, retaining some ridges and irregularities. Blend and conceal the joint with clay if you've added a piece of neck.

5 Add dimensional accents with a toothpick or other sharp implement. Incise small cracks and rows of adobe brick that seem to stand behind cracked stucco. Create a small "rug" by applying additional clay to the surface. Use a small piece of cloth as a model to create folds and wrinkles, and make the rug's shape somewhat irregular, so it seems to drape across the gourd. Press some coarse cloth into the damp clay to leave a woven impression. Cut small decorative designs into the rug, or paint them on later.

6 Create tiny pieces of "pottery" using small jewelry-size gourds. In this example, I created two pots from one miniature bottle gourd, and a plate from a small gourd scrap. Make shallow impressions in the damp clay of the rug by pressing the pottery pieces gently into it (you will glue the pots into these depressions later). Remove the pots from the damp clay, wipe off any clay that adheres to them, and set them aside.

7 Allow the clay to dry thoroughly; touch up small cracks with additional clay at any time during the drying process. Temperature and humidity affect the drying time, but overnight is usually sufficient. You'll find the gourd is surprisingly light when the clay is dry.

ADDING TEXTURAL ELEMENTS

8 Using a sponge, paint the gourd with thin layers of earthy colors to achieve a final coat that is slightly mottled and uneven. When this base is totally dry, use a wash of watered-down dark brown paint to highlight cracks and depressions. For best results, work one small area and then another, until you treat the entire surface. Apply the wash, then remove most of it with a clean damp sponge, leaving small amounts only in cracks and crevices.

> **TIP:** If you prefer, find commercially made textural paints at most craft and hardware stores. These products come in spray and brush-on formulas, and each gives a slightly different finished look.

9 Paint the rug and the pottery pieces. When completely dry, glue the pottery pieces into their preformed depressions.

10 Drill tiny holes around the top edge of the gourd's neck and glue in small pieces of dowel or toothpick to create mock beams piercing the stucco. Trim them, and paint them dark brown after the glue sets.

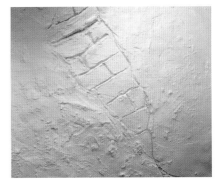

Cracked stucco and rows of "brick" give your piece more character. Add these details with a sharp tool.

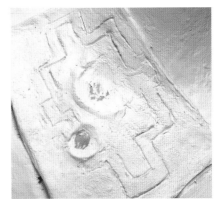

Fashion a "rug" from the wet clay. Small depressions mark where the pots will be glued.

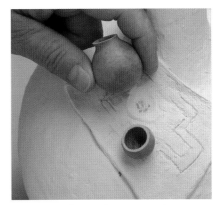

Press a small gourd "pot" into the wet clay to create a depression. Paint the pot and glue it into the small depression.

Many tiny parts work together to create a big impression in this enchanting piece of pottery, including a handmade kiva ladder, pots, a rug, and "beams" made from wooden dowel.

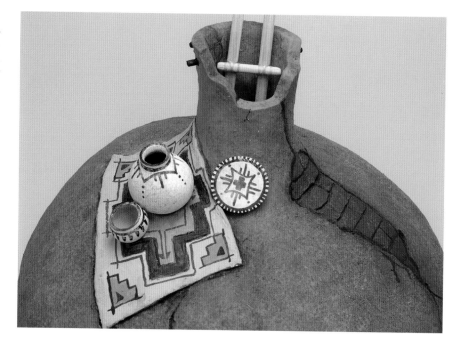

11 Create a ladder for your pottery with lengths of dowel or scrap pine. Lay the two outer structural pieces on a flat surface. Make them slightly different lengths, and place them at an angle so the base is a bit wider than the top (make sure the ladder's base is narrower than the gourd's opening, or it won't fit). Attach a few rungs made from smaller pieces of dowel, using wood glue. Three to five crosspieces are sufficient, depending on the ladder's length. When the glue is set, tie artificial sinew or other cord around where each rung meets the sides. This is a nice decorative touch that gives the ladder greater strength.

12 Spray the completed pottery with a clear matte or satin sealer.

SCULPTURAL RAINSTICK

The "maiden" figure is reminiscent of southwestern native cultures, where pottery vessels are both artistic and utilitarian elements in pueblo life. The figure here—a functional rainstick, as well as a striking sculpture—carries a large pottery plate and balances a water olla (container) atop her head. Rotate it gently back and forth to enjoy its soothing rain-like sound.

Materials

- snake or club gourd, cleaned
- small gourds or gourd pieces suitable for face and pottery shapes
- chicken wire
- rice, glass beads, beans, or other rainmaking materials
- 1 inch (25 mm) pine or ⅛ inch (3 mm) basswood
- small dowel pieces
- wood glue
- acrylic paints, metallic patina paints (optional)
- clear spray sealer (matte or semigloss)
- embellishments of your choice (antler slices, beads, feathers)

Tools

- small keyhole handsaw or mini-jigsaw
- tin snips or wire cutters
- hand file or sandpaper
- paintbrush, sponge, and dye applicator (optional)

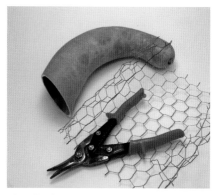

The chief components of the rainstick are a snake gourd and a roll of chicken wire.

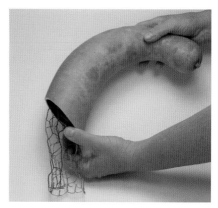

Roll the chicken wire loosely and insert it into the gourd. The loosely-rolled wire allows small noisemaking objects to pass around and through it.

CREATING A SIMPLE RAINSTICK

1 Cut a snake or club gourd straight across or on a slant, to make the completed figure stand at an interesting angle. Remove all the seeds and pulp from the gourd's interior.

2 Cut a section of chicken wire slightly shorter than the gourd and wide enough that you can roll it loosely into a tube. Roll the wire loosely so the "rainmaking" objects will hit the wire and pass through as the rainstick is manipulated. Insert the rolled tube into the gourd.

3 Experiment with a variety of materials—rice, beans, beads, small stones, and others—to see which makes the most pleasing sound. Cover the end of the gourd with your hand as you rotate it to hear the sound of each. The example here contains a mixture of rice and glass beads of different sizes.

4 Plug the bottom of the gourd with a wooden stopper made from scrap pine, or cover it with a piece of thin basswood. The wood plug has the advantage of adding weight to the base for stability.

Trace around the base of the gourd to make a template for the plug. Cut the plug from the scrap pine, and shape and fit the plug, using a belt sander, hand files, or other tools, as necessary. Taper the plug slightly so it fits snugly inside the gourd. Add the rainmaking material to the gourd. Coat the edges of the finished plug with glue and insert it into the base. Prop the

Add rice or beads to the gourd as "rainmakers." Test to be sure you like the sound before gluing on the base.

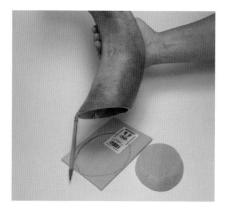

Make a base or plug to fit, using either a thick wood plug inserted into the gourd, or a flat wood base that's glued onto the bottom.

gourd upside-down so the rainmaking objects fall to the far end of the gourd, away from the wet glue. When the glue is dry, file or sand the base to make the cut edge of the gourd flush with the wooden plug. Fill any small gaps with filler.

For an exterior stopper, trace the template onto a piece of thin basswood. Cut, test fit, and glue this piece to the bottom of the gourd. Be sure to add the rainmaking objects before you glue on the base. When the glue is dry, sand and smooth the margins where the cut gourd meets the basswood base.

ADDING THE MASK AND POTTERY ACCENTS

5 Select small gourds or gourd pieces for the mask and pottery accents. A small bottle gourd makes an attractive pot, and small gourd scraps work well for the mask and shallow dish.

Alternate sanding and test fitting the mask until it sits snugly against the gourd. Glue the mask in place and use masking tape to hold it firmly until the glue is set. Create a "mouth" for the mask, using a small piece of dowel; drill through the mask and the underlying gourd, and glue in a short section of ¼-inch (6-mm) dowel. The dowel mouth should extend only about ¼ inch (6 mm) out from the front of the mask. When the glue is dry, burn or drill a small round depression in the center of the dowel.

Create a small pot to rest on the maiden's head. Make the pot from a scrap gourd top or piece cut from a small gourd.

Flatten the top of the rainstick (the maiden's head) and the bottom of the gourd pot, using a file or sandpaper. Strengthen the joint between the pot and the head by drilling holes in the top of the head and the bottom of the pot. Glue a short piece of dowel into the hole at the bottom of the pot, and set the pot aside; you'll attach it after the painting is complete.

Grind or sand the inside of the small dish-shape piece, and shape the outside to conform to the curve of the gourd body. Drill shallow holes in the backside of the dish and in the gourd body, and glue a short piece of dowel in the back of the dish. Set the dish aside.

> **TIP:** Use these directions to make a variety of gourd rainsticks. Add arms and a flute to create a Kokopelli figure, or a brightly painted headdress, or tableta, to make a butterfly maiden. Or try a completely different direction, and make the rainstick figure Asian or African.

Prepare the gourd mask, pot, and bowl accents.

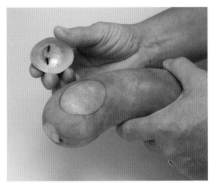

Test fit and glue the mask onto the rainstick.

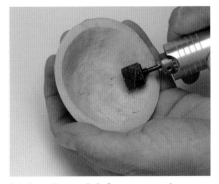

Make a large dish from a gourd scrap. Sand the interior of the dish to create a smooth surface for painting, and the exterior of the dish to ensure a strong bond when you glue it to the rainstick.

PAINTING AND FINISHING THE FIGURE

6 Explore your creativity in this step. Paint the figure as shown (with designs from the Zuni Pueblo), or use another southwestern design. The plate and olla's elaborate designs contrast strikingly with the relative simplicity of the patina-painted body (see complete directions for a genuine patina finish in Lidded Bowl with Antler Handle, page 134).

When the painting is complete, glue the pot and dish on the gourd body with the dowels. Finish with a matte or semigloss sealer. Add feathers, bone, or other accents, if desired.

VARIATION

The same basic construction steps produce this rainstick, which features very different finishes and embellishments.

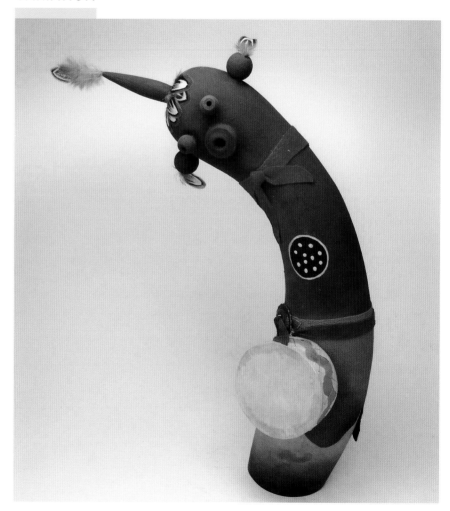

BIRD EFFIGY POTTERY

Beginning in prehistory, cultures around the world produced vessels in the shape of (or displaying) figures, often fish, birds, and other small animals; the significance of the creatures depicted in this "effigy pottery" varied from one culture to another. Now you can create your own bird effigy from gourds and scrap pieces.

Materials

- small gourd, cleaned
- gourd neck piece and scraps
- water-based wood filler
- acrylic paints
- twisted sea grass or other decorative cording
- ¼-inch (6-mm) dowel
- wood glue
- flat black spray paint
- clear spray sealer (matte or semigloss)

Tools

- pencil
- small handsaw or mini-jigsaw
- paper towel
- drill and ¼-inch (6-mm) drill bit (brad point, optional)
- sandpaper or files
- artist's sea sponge
- small paintbrush

SELECTING AND PREPARING THE GOURD

1 Select a small cannonball, dipper, or canteen gourd. If you wish the piece to have a neck or head, leave part of the natural gourd neck, or add a gourd scrap.

2 Cut the gourd and clean the interior thoroughly. Sand the cut edge to smooth and level the opening. File or sand the bottom of the gourd, if necessary, to make it sit level. If desired, spray the gourd interior with flat black paint.

3 If you're adding a neck and/or head, select a suitable gourd scrap. Choose a piece proportionate to the body—straight, curved, or twisted in any manner—and trim it to an appropriate length.

An assortment of small round gourds, neck pieces, and scraps are the basic components of the effigy.

PRECISION FITTING MULTIPLE GOURD PIECES

Test fit the neck piece to the gourd body, and lightly mark the position with pencil so you can later glue the neck in the same spot. Mark areas on the neck that seem high, and sand or file as needed to achieve a reasonable fit. In many cases, the simple angling of the neck's inside edge will do it, but it may take repeated sanding and testing to ensure a good contact.

This simple means of joining pieces is a "butt joint," the least strong of all woodworking joints. The surface area contact alone determines the bond's strength. While wood filler can eliminate small gaps, the essential strength of the joint is good close contact between the parts. Attach the neck with wood glue, and tape or hold in place until the glue is set.

> **TIP:** When unusual or curving shapes make gluing pieces difficult, use a combination of glues. Coat the major part of the area with wood glue, and add a drop of fast-setting gap-filling cyanoacrylate in a few places. The CA glue sets very quickly to hold the parts in place while the wood glue dries. When cured, the wood glue will provide an even stronger bond.

When the glue is dry, give the bird a beak: drill a ¼-inch (6-mm) hole into the head and insert a short length of ¼-inch (6-mm) dowel. Shape the dowel in a pencil sharpener or trim it with a hobby knife, then sand it smooth. After test fitting, cement the piece with wood glue.

4 Create a tail piece of any shape, and make it curved or flat. Cut the piece with a small tenon or tongue on the end, where you'll join it to the body. A sizable piece to be joined by a small surface area calls for a mortise and tenon, a very strong woodworking joint. While sounding complicated, this joint is actually very simple, and provides a solid, durable bond; it's basically a tongue, or tenon, inserted into a precut slot, or mortise.

Holding the tail piece in the desired location on the gourd, trace around the tongue to mark the spot. Ensure the tail mortise is level and directly opposite the neck, and keep in mind that the tail's height (how high or low you place it) affects the angle at which it projects from the gourd. Placed higher on the gourd, the tail will point up; placed lower, it will stick out straight.

Cut inside your guide line; you can always enlarge the cut to fit. When the fit is tight, join the pieces with wood glue, and set aside until the glue is dry.

5 Add small handles with a simple butt joint, reinforced with tiny dowel-like pieces of toothpick. If you take the time to ensure a good fit, the reinforcing dowels are usually unnecessary.

Drill the handles through the center with a ¼-inch (6-mm) drill bit. A brad-point bit works especially well: The brad point creates a pilot hole and keeps the bit from drifting on the surface. It's easier to drill the hole in a large scrap first, then cut the handle shape around the hole. Place a scrap of gourd on a wood block and drill through the scrap and slightly into the underlying wood. This prevents the bit from damaging the handle's underside as it cuts through.

Add a curving neckpiece to the gourd, and cut small pieces for the handles.

Wood filler disguises the joint where parts have been attached. Use a damp paper towel to smooth the filler.

Cut a slot in the body of the gourd, shaped to match the curve of the tail section to be added.

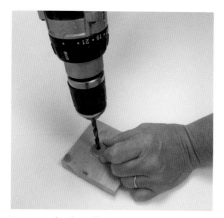

Position the handle pieces atop a wood scrap to prevent damage as you drill them.

The "bird" now has a wood dowel beak and handles. The joints are filled, and the surface is smooth and ready for painting.

6 When the pieces are joined and the glue is set, fill small gaps or flaws with wood filler. Reduce the need for sanding later by smoothing the filler with a damp finger or wet piece of paper towel. Rub the filler gently with fine sandpaper or a damp towel even after it's dry to refine the finish.

DECORATING THE EFFIGY

7 Paint the pot with acrylics, which cover and disguise the joints. Prehistoric potters generally used solid color clay and scant embellishment, but modern effigy pieces often have geometric southwestern designs. Paint your creation however you like.

The example here has acrylic paint sponged on in thin layers, in shades of white. Apply the whitewash with an artist's sponge, building layers to cover the joints, but allowing some of the gourd surface to show through.

Add rustic-looking designs with black or rust-colored paint; cover the pot's entire surface or only select areas, such as the head and tail. Look at photographs or reference material on prehistoric or modern Pueblo pottery for additional color and pattern ideas.

As a final touch, gently blot the entire surface of the gourd with a sponge dipped in thinned white paint to mute the painted design and add the appearance of age.

8 Spray the completed pottery with clear matte sealer.

9 Add a handle made from sea grass, often used for weaving baskets, or other rustic-looking cord or raffia.

VARIATIONS

Alternative designs and decorations for effigy pottery.

HOPI DRAGONFLY VESSEL

Native cultures of the Southwest have long associations with beautiful, functional works of art. This interpretation of two traditional Hopi crafts blends a stylized dragonfly and woven rain cloud symbols. Try your hand at creating an appealing vessel that combines gourd "pottery" and coiled basketry.

Materials

- gourd, cleaned
- flat black spray paint
- air-dry clay
- acrylic paints (colors that blend with the selected waxed linen cord)
- clear spray finish (matte)
- white glue
- waxed linen cord (suggested colors: oatmeal/natural, black, light rust, and either light yellow or pale green)
- weaving core material, one of the following: ⁵⁄₃₂ inch (4 mm) fiber rush or twisted paper cord, size 5 or 6 round basketry reed, or vinyl-coated clothesline cording

Tools

- small handsaw or mini-jigsaw
- hand file and/or sandpaper
- artist's sea sponge
- small paintbrush
- awl
- masking tape or thin quilter's marking tape (optional)
- drill and a ¹⁄₁₆-inch (1.6-mm) drill bit
- scissors or craft knife
- blunted tapestry needles

CUTTING AND PREPARING THE GOURD

1 Draw a straight, level line around the gourd, near the top. Cut the gourd with a mini-jigsaw or handsaw, and file or sand the cut edge at a slight inward angle.

2 Clean the gourd interior thoroughly, removing all the pulp.

3 Spray the interior with flat black enamel spray, or whitewash it with thinned-down acrylic paint of the same color that will be used to paint the exterior.

MARKING AND DRILLING HOLES

4 Divide the cut edge of the gourd into four equal sections and mark them in pencil. Mark each quadrant at its midpoint, and halve and mark each of these sections in turn. Continue dividing thus until the marks are approximately ½ to ¾ inch (12 to 18 mm) apart. The number of divisions will vary with the gourd's size. Another option is to run a thin strip of masking or quilter's tape around the top of the gourd until the ends just meet. Lay the tape flat and use a ruler to divide the strip into equal segments, the number of which must be divisible by 4. Replace the tape and transfer the marks to the gourd rim.

5 Measure ³⁄₁₆ inch (5 mm) down from the gourd's rim, and use an awl to bore starter holes at each of the marks made in the step above. This piercing makes drilling easier and more accurate. Keep the drill perpendicular to the surface as you make each hole.

FINISHING THE EXTERIOR

6 Draw the dragonfly pattern on the gourd, or several dragonflies, if you choose. Smear a little white glue over the dragonfly outline to give the clay a better bond. Press air-dry clay on the area, flattening and shaping it with damp fingers. Trim the excess clay as needed with a craft knife. Smooth

Numbers 1 through 4 show the initial divisions, and small marks between them indicate further divisions. Section A (the upper right quadrant) has eight divisions marked. The four dots to the right of the number 1 indicate the width of the pattern repeat.

the edges of the finished dragonfly with damp fingers. Etch a design into the wet clay, if you like, or carve one into the clay after it dries. When you finish, set the gourd aside until the clay is dry.

Some slight cracking is normal during drying; if any cracks develop, press a bit of fresh clay into them. When the clay is completely dry, sand it lightly to refine the surface.

Sculpt a dragonfly on the gourd, using air-dry clay. Any brand of air-dry clay works well for sculpting on gourds.

7 Lightly paint the gourd exterior, using a sponge and acrylic paint that is similar in color to the oatmeal waxed linen. Allow some of the gourd's natural color to show through the paint. Add faint accents of light rust and metallic paint, as desired. Paint the dragonfly a light rust, and then lightly sponge a faint trace of the oatmeal color over it.

8 Seal the paint when dry with a matte spray finish.

CREATING A COILED BASKETRY WEAVE

Follow the basket weaving pattern shown, or draw and develop your own, using graph paper. The pattern given repeats properly when the number of holes is divisible by 4; be sure to make adjustments if you change either the design or the number of holes.

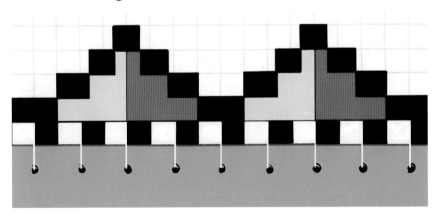

Basket Weaving Pattern

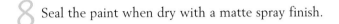

The painted and sealed gourd bowl has a ring of holes around the rim, through which the coiling will attach.

9 Cut a piece of the oatmeal waxed linen cord about 3 to 4 feet (1 to 1½ m) in length, and thread it through a blunt tapestry needle. Avoid the temptation to use a longer piece: the cord may tangle or fray, and you can easily add new lengths as you work. Cut one end of the coil core material at an angle with a scissors or craft knife. Hold it on the rim of the gourd so the angled end is just above one of the drilled holes.

> **TIP:** I find it easiest to place the core material to the left so it is worked around the gourd in a clockwise direction. This way I can hold the excess material in my left hand, while wrapping the coils with my right hand. Stitching from front to back will make it easier to see each stitch. You'll obviously reverse these directions if you're left handed.

Place the threaded needle through the hole just below the core material. Draw the cord through until only a short tail remains on the outside of the gourd. Pull the tail over the top to the back side of the core, and secure it in place by stitching a second time through the same hole. Continue wrapping around the core and any remaining tail until it's time to add a new color or to stitch through the next hole.

The first row of coiling and stitching is off to a good start. Notice the black cord being wrapped along with the core and carried until it's needed.

10 Add the second color (in this case, black) several stitches before it's needed. Place the black cord behind the core with the long end lying in the same direction as the core material. Wrap the oatmeal cord around both the core and the black cord until the new piece of cord is secure. When it's time to change colors, pull the black thread forward and wrap it around both the core and the oatmeal cord. Carry one or more extra colors along as the coil is being wrapped, and switch colors as needed. At times, you'll be wrapping with one color and carrying up to three others behind the coil. Add new lengths of cord in this manner. Continue to wrap the coil like this until you reach the beginning point, where you'll begin the second row.

11 Join the coils of subsequent rows together using a figure-eight locking stitch. Bring the cord over the top coil as before; thread it between the coils, and then reverse the direction to encircle the lower coil (see drawing below right). Pull the cord firmly to blend it into the row below. When the two rows are different colors, hide the lower stitch by wrapping the bottom coil in the appropriate color, using the cord carried along behind the coil. Continue coiling in this manner until the pattern is finished.

12 To finish the basket, cut and angle the core material so it ends directly above the point where the coiling began. Wrap the final portion of the core and blend the final stitches into the top edge of the basket.

Adding the second row of coiling. Several colors are carried behind the weaving.

MEDICINE WHEEL BASKET

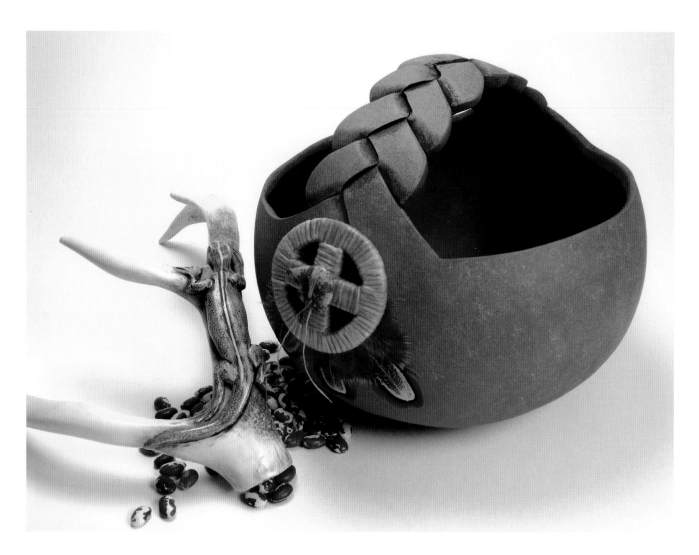

The medicine wheel is widely used in Native American cultures as a symbol of life, the universe, and the directions of life's journey. This simple, elegant gourd basket has a braided handle with medicine wheel accents. Finish the basket with a braided handle made by burning or carving; burning the handle is quick and easy, while carving adds dimension and realism.

Materials

- kettle or bushel basket gourd, cleaned
- acrylic paints, leather dye (optional)
- flat black spray paint or leather dye
- clear finish (matte)
- artificial sinew or other lacing material
- embellishments of your choice (antler slices, beads, feathers)

Tools

- small keyhole handsaw or mini-jigsaw
- hand file or sandpaper
- paintbrush, sponge, and dye applicator (optional)
- wood-burning tool or rotary tool, carving burs, and sanding drum
- awl or drill

CUTTING AND CLEANING THE GOURD

1 On the shell of the selected gourd, mark where you want the top edge of the basket to be. Draw the braided handle design on the gourd, using the patterns shown on page 114. Adjust the handle length as needed by adding or removing right or left (center) sections of the pattern. Flip the end sections of the pattern as needed to fit.

2 Cut the gourd with a mini-jigsaw or handsaw, using care when cutting around the curved braids. Smooth the cut edges with a hand file and sandpaper.

3 Clean the gourd interior thoroughly, and color it with spray enamel or leather dye.

The gourd basket, after having been marked and cut.

Medicine Wheel Basket Patterns

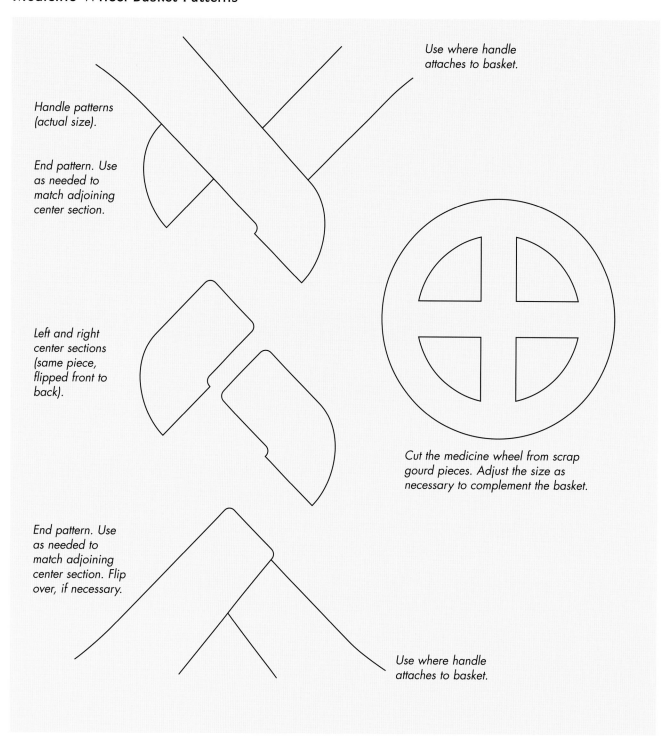

Use where handle attaches to basket.

Handle patterns (actual size).

End pattern. Use as needed to match adjoining center section.

Left and right center sections (same piece, flipped front to back).

Cut the medicine wheel from scrap gourd pieces. Adjust the size as necessary to complement the basket.

End pattern. Use as needed to match adjoining center section. Flip over, if necessary.

Use where handle attaches to basket.

WOOD BURNING OR CARVING A BRAIDED HANDLE

4 Burn or carve the handle, depending on your level of skill and the time you wish to invest in the project.

To wood burn the handle, first burn all the lines of the pattern. Next, burn shadows in the areas where the braids cross. Lay your tool flat to do this, and burn with the side of the tip. Burn deeply to add dimension. This technique is most effective on gourds retaining their natural, unpainted finish.

To carve the handle, cut all the lines of the pattern, using a rotary tool and an inverted cone or small cylinder bur. Hold the tool so the side of the bur does the cutting. Carve shadows by excising a bit of the gourd where the braid sections cross. This contouring makes the sections appear to cross around each other. When the carving is complete, smooth it with a drum sander, and hand sand to finish. A light mist of spray sealer on the carved surfaces prevents them from soaking up finishes later at a faster rate than the surrounding surfaces. Wipe away any excess spray with a rag while still damp.

5 Leave the basket finish natural, or color it with dye, paint, or another agent. I treated the example here with a light base of leather dye, followed by thin coats of paint in tans and browns sponged on for a leather-like appearance. Be sure to experiment on scrap material first with any new product or method to make sure you will like the results. Seal and finish painted or dyed surfaces with a matte or semigloss spray; substitute paste wax or tung oil on unpainted gourd surfaces.

CREATING A MEDICINE WHEEL EMBELLISHMENT FROM SCRAP

6 Cut two circular discs from the scrap pieces removed from the handle area. Trace around a cylindrical object or draw a circle with a compass in a size that complements your basket. Draw a second, slightly smaller circle inside, and add a cross bar in the shape of an X. Make the outer wheel and inner spokes the same width. Cut out the circles and the four wedges of the wheel by drilling starter holes first, and then sawing with a mini-jigsaw or keyhole saw.

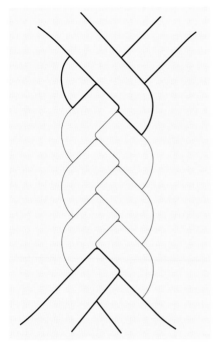

The assembled pattern pieces form a basket handle, here showing the areas to be carved and shaded.

Wood burn the handle with the side of the burner tip to shade and contour the braid.

Wrap the medicine wheel with artificial sinew or other lacing material, following the process shown here.

Attach the medicine wheel to the basket handle area by lacing through holes already drilled into the gourd.

7 Wrap the wheels with artificial sinew or other material. Wrap the outer circle first, just to the side of a spoke; wrap closely, allowing little of the underlying gourd to show through. Fold the tail end of the sinew under as you work, so the wrapping covers and holds it in place; do the same with further lengths of sinew as you add them. When you reach a crossbar, wrap the sinew around and over the entire wheel until the spoke is covered. Continue around the perimeter until you reach the second crossbar, and wrap across the entire wheel again. Once the outer wheel is completely covered, wrap the inner spokes in the same manner. When the wheel is completely covered, tie the loose ends of sinew around the wheel's center in the back, or use a needle to weave them under.

8 Position one of the completed wheels on the gourd where the braided handle meets the bowl. Make four small holes, one at each corner of the square in the center formed by the crossing spokes, using an awl or drill. Sew the wheel onto the basket through the holes, using a short length of sinew to make an X pattern across the center. Knot, clip, or add beads to the loose ends of sinew. Repeat on the other side of the basket with the second wheel.

9 Glue some small feathers under the wheel, and tie fetishes or beads onto the center of it. These added embellishments give the basket your personal stamp. Have fun doing it!

Choose from a variety of embellishments to trim the basket.

RIPPLES AND STREAMS

Carved "sand ripples," inlaid bead strands, and gold leaf lend dazzling effects to a gourd. Each technique is impressive by itself, but together, what a masterpiece!

Creating dimensional ripples that flow gracefully around a gourd provides an excellent lesson in the basic principles and techniques of power carving. Take your carving skills a step further, and cut a channel for inlay. With a bit of practice, you'll soon feel very much at home using a rotary tool, and you'll know the satisfaction of having inlaid the beads and added the gold-leafed "streams" yourself.

Ripples and Streams. *This project offers options in the size and purpose of your gourd creation. Choose from a small candle-holder or a larger vessel, both featuring a splendid variety of techniques.*

Materials

- kettle, canteen, or small pear-shape gourd, cleaned
- acrylic paints
- gold leaf
- water-based gold leaf size (adhesive)
- clear spray lacquer
- clear spray finish (matte or semigloss)
- water-based clear sealer (gloss)
- flat black spray paint
- gap-filling cyanoacrylate glue
- heishi or seed beads, strung

Optional Materials and Tools

- glass oil lamp insert with wick holder and wick
- clean-burning lamp oil
- drill with ⅝-inch (16-mm) drill bit (brad point, optional)

Tools

- small handsaw or jigsaw
- flat or half-round hand file
- round riffler file
- sandpaper (medium and fine grits)
- burning tool (optional)
- rotary tool (wheel, ball, and inverted cone burs, and sanding drum)
- small detail paintbrush
- artist's sea sponge
- old paintbrush for applying adhesive
- old flat paintbrush with stiff bristles for smoothing gold leaf

SELECTING AND PREPARING THE GOURD

1 You can make this project in a variety of sizes; decide first how big you want to make it. For a small candleholder, choose a pear-shape gourd about 5 inches (13 cm) tall. Cut or drill a ⅝-inch (16-mm) hole at the top of the gourd; use a brad-point wood bit, or drill a small pilot hole first to prevent the larger drill from "walking" about on the gourd's rounded surface. If you don't have a suitable drill bit, make the hole with a smaller one, or cut the hole with a small saw. Use a rotary tool and a drum sander to enlarge the hole little by little until the candle insert slips in easily.

> **TIP:** Gourd crafting supply dealers, craft stores, and some wood-working suppliers offer small glass oil-candle inserts. These small glass inserts are imperative for burning candles safely. Never use a gourd as a candleholder without a protective glass insert.

Make a larger vessel from any size gourd. Cut an opening of any size at the top of the gourd. Smooth the cut edges with a hand file or sandpaper.

2 Clean the gourd interior thoroughly. For a large gourd, remove all pulp residue and spray the interior with matte black paint.

The small opening in the candleholder gourd makes it very difficult to remove all the pulp. Use a dowel, small round file, or other slender tool to break up the seed ball as much as possible. Shake out the loose material, and repeat as needed until the candle insert seats properly in the gourd. Removing every last bit of pulp isn't critical; just be sure to remove all the loose material.

DRAWING YOUR DESIGN

3 Draw the ripples on the gourd. Use a pencil to draw and design, and keep a damp cloth or baby wipe handy to remove stray marks. Start the lines at the top of the gourd and draw them all the way to the bottom, curving gently into very shallow S curves. Gentle curves are much easier to carve than tight ones. Visualize wind-blown ripples in the sand, undulating gently as they move across the surface.

Make the lines no closer than ½ inch (12 mm) apart at the top of the gourd, and spread and widen them as they move around the fat belly of the gourd. Draw the lines together again and narrow them slightly as they reach the bottom of the gourd.

Odd numbers are the most visually interesting, and three or five ripples are usually enough to constitute the overall design. Draw one line more than the total number of ripples you desire; for example, four drawn lines produce three ripples. Allow at least two-thirds of the gourd's surface to remain flat, without ripples.

4 Next, draw a pair of wavy lines near the bottom third of the gourd to suggest a stream. Draw these lines horizontally in the flat area, beginning at one ripple line and continuing around the gourd to the far ripple. Undulate the lines; don't match them and don't space them evenly. The section between the wavy lines should curve gently, representing a flowing stream that might produce ripples in the sand.

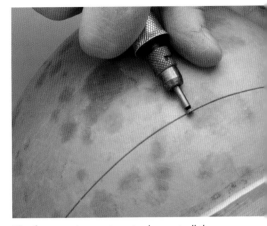

The first step in carving ripples: cut all the lines with a narrow-diameter wheel bur.

CARVING DIMENSIONAL "RIPPLES"

TIP: For a better understanding of the carving techniques that follow, be sure to read about carving tools and techniques on pages 27–32.

5 The first step in carving the ripples is to cut the lines you've drawn, using a rotary tool and wheel-shape bur. Use a wheel with a narrow diameter to keep it from penetrating the gourd shell, even when cutting to its full depth. The ideal is a wheel bur approximately 5/32 inch (4 mm) in diameter, but it can be hard to find. The best sources for tools in hard-to-find sizes are hobby shops, specialty woodworking stores, and gourd crafting tool suppliers.

Cut a groove along each of the lines you've drawn to define the ripples. This small groove delineates the side of each ripple, and will provide a cut to follow in the next step.

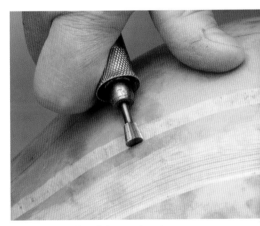

Make one side of the cut line lower, using an inverted cone bur.

6 Reduce (make lower) one side of each ripple by carving along one side of the groove you cut with the wheel bur. It doesn't matter which side of the groove you lower; just make it the same side for each ripple. Right-handed people will find it easier to cut the right side of each groove.

Use an inverted cone bur, and place the edge of the bur directly into the groove. While cutting, the bur will track along the groove; this two-step process makes a cleaner, neater cut than an inverted cone can produce by itself.

The overall thickness of the gourd will determine the amount to be cut

A hand file evens out the ripples' bumps and ridges.

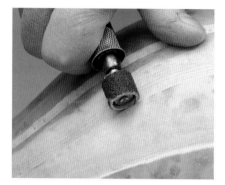

Smooth the reduced areas of the ripples with a drum sander, blending them into the surrounding uncut surfaces.

Use a small riffler file to smooth and even out the cut edges of the ripples.

away. Very thick gourds can bear deep, dramatic ripples; cut thinner gourds more shallowly. Reduce the shell most deeply at the groove and let the ripple swell gradually as it moves over the body of the gourd. Cut each ripple in the same manner until all have been made lower along one side.

7 Your carving will probably be somewhat bumpy and uneven the first time you try it. Don't despair; it's easy to smooth the surface. Use a hand file to flatten out the ridges and bumps from carving, or sand the area with a drum sander. Apply these techniques in combination, and minimal hand sanding—the next step—will finish the job.

Remove remaining tool marks with a hand sander, using a strip of sandpaper cut from a 1-inch- (2.5-cm-) wide sanding belt. Sanding belts have a much heavier cloth backing, and unlike conventional sandpaper, maintain a sharp edge even with long-term use.

Sand with finer and finer sandpaper until the surface of each ripple is smooth and blends evenly into the surrounding uncut area of the ripple.

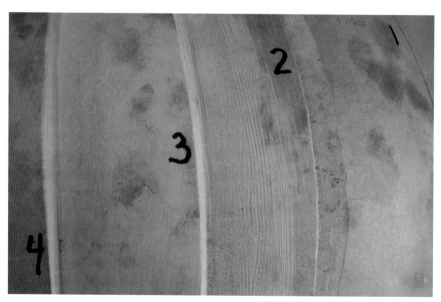

The progression in carving the ripples, from the initial cut to the finished surface.

8 Cut a small offset at the top of each ripple for an attractive (optional) rim treatment. Cut a short line down the side of each ripple (see photo at right); then cut downward diagonally across each ripple to the adjacent ripple. Sand and smooth the cut edges, and spray them again with flat black paint.

Cut the top edge of the gourd, if you like, into a decorative pattern, for added interest. Cut downward at an angle across the top of each ripple.

CARVING A CHANNEL TO INLAY BEADS

9 Cut a channel to inlay heishi (pronounced he'-shee, meaning "shell") beads along the top line of the "stream." Cut the upper line first with a narrow-diameter wheel bur, as you did the ripples. Cut the lower line of the stream with the wheel bur, or burn it with a wood-burning tool.

10 Next, follow along the same groove with a ball-shape bur, keeping the ball centered in the middle of the channel. For better control, cut the channel in several shallow passes rather than a single deep one. Use a ball bur the same approximate diameter as the beads to be inlaid. If necessary, make the channel uniform and even in width and depth by filing with a round riffler.

File the finished channel to exactly half the depth of the beads you plan to inlay; the inlaid beads must sit precisely half above the gourd surface, and half below. Glue in the beads only *after* the gourd is painted and finished.

TIP: Use pre-strung size 10 or 12 seed beads, or 2- to 3-mm heishi strands for this type of inlay. Available in a wide variety of colors, pre-strung beads are quicker and easier to apply. Heishi beads were originally made only from natural shell, but are available now in a larger palette of colors and materials. Their tubular shape makes heishi look almost seamless in this type of channel inlay.

Cut the heishi inlay channel first with a wheel bur; enlarge it in the next step with a ball bur.

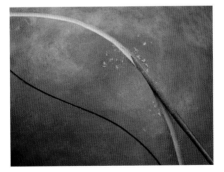

Even out the inlay channel with a small round riffler file to a uniform depth and width.

Use the darkest tones for the sand ripples' first coat of paint.

Sponge additional layers of paint on the ripples in successively lighter colors to add highlights and the appearance of depth.

PAINTING AND FINISHING

11 Before painting, mist the sand ripple area very lightly with lacquer spray. This coating seals the carved surface to prevent its swelling or becoming rough with the application of paint.

12 Paint the gourd using acrylic paints and an artist's sea sponge, beginning with the rippled area. The ripples can be painted in any colors, but using shades of brown, tan, or related colors will be the most suggestive of actual sand.

The skillful addition of paint heightens the effect of depth and dimension in the ripples. First, apply a layer of dark brown paint in the most deeply recessed part of each groove. Add a second layer, using a similar but lighter shade of brown. Be sure that some of the darkest brown paint shows through the new layer, especially in the deepest recesses of the ripple. Sponge on additional layers of paint, gradually lightening the shade of both the paint and the ripple as you approach the opposite edge of the ripple. Add some sparkle to the ripples by sponging on a final thin application of metallic paint.

13 Paint the base of the gourd in a color of your choice, using a sponge. Use a darker tone on the base, reserving lighter ones for the gourd's upper section. Several similar shades of color endows greater depth to the paint's finished appearance, and a bit of metallic paint as the final layer makes it pop. Don't worry about any paint that accidentally overlaps the stream design; the gold leaf will cover it.

14 Paint the upper section of the gourd in a lighter shade, allowing some of the gourd surface to show through. Pay special attention to the area abutting the ripples; blend this area carefully into the larger uncarved surface. Add small petroglyphs, Native American figures, or any design you like, using a fine brush and a light color.

When you finish the painting, cut a series of decorative dots in the dark painted area at the base of the gourd. Use a rotary tool with a ball-shape bur, and cut a flowing line of shallow dots along, and just under, the margin of the stream.

15 Spray the entire gourd with a coat of matte or semigloss finish.

APPLYING GOLD LEAF

16 After the finish coat has dried, add gold leaf to accent the stream. Apply a coat of gold leaf adhesive size to the entire stream area, using an old brush. Rub a bit of dish soap into the bristles of the brush before dipping it into the adhesive; this makes it easier to clean the adhesive from the brush later.

Adhesive size is milky in appearance when wet, but dries to a tacky, clear finish. Wait until the adhesive size turns clear before you apply the gold leaf; this may take up to an hour, depending on the temperature and humidity. To avoid a gummy mess, never add the gold leaf before the size is completely dry.

Gold leaf is sold in small "books" containing five to 25 leaves. Genuine gold leaf is very expensive, but craft quality imitation leaf (known as "composition leaf" or "Dutch metal leaf") looks great and is easy to find at reasonable prices. These kinds of craft leafing material come in a variety of colors, including gold, silver, and copper, as well as in variegated and patterned styles.

Place a sheet of leafing material on top of the dried adhesive. Carefully press the leaf onto the surface, using clean fingers or a soft brush. Continue to apply the leafing until you cover the entire stream area. Gently tear away any excess leaf that extends beyond the adhesive, for use in another area. Touch up any small areas where the leaf did not adhere well by coating it again with adhesive size. Let the size fully dry, and patch the areas with little pieces of brushed-away leaf (known as "skewings").

Use a flat brush with stiff bristles to brush away all the excess leaf. Save the skewings in a small container for repairs or use in other projects. Lightly polish the leaf with a soft cloth, rubbing gently in a circular motion.

Brush a finish coat of clear gloss sealer over the leafing to protect the surface and prevent tarnishing. Be aware that some brands of gloss finish may dull or change the accent colors on variegated leaf; test the finish on a scrap of leaf before applying it to the finished gourd.

17 Glue the heishi or seed beads into the channel. For the best results, use gap-filling cyanoacrylate; it's more viscous than the superglue most hardware stores carry, and you can find it in craft and hobby stores. The thicker gap-filling consistency allows the glue to sit on the surface of the channel, and not soak immediately into the gourd. This type of glue has a very fine applicator tip. Run the tip down the length of the channel, applying a consistent bead of glue. If necessary, use a toothpick to spread the glue evenly. For very long inlays, don't glue the entire channel at once—work in smaller sections. Take care not to apply too much glue; the excess can squeeze out of the channel and look unsightly. It doesn't take much glue to hold the beads in place.

Apply gold leaf adhesive size with an old brush. The size will turn clear as it dries.

The gold leaf is applied. The example uses variegated gold leaf.

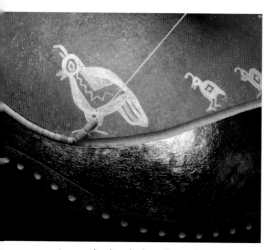

Leave the heishi beads on the string when you glue them into the prepared channel, using gap-filling superglue.

Starting at the end of the channel, place one end of the strand of beads into the groove. Continue adding beads, allowing no gaps between them. Press the beads firmly into the glued groove. When the channel is filled, trim the bead string at both ends.

If you plan to use the gourd with an oil candle insert, use a good quality, clean-burning lamp oil. For safe burning, carefully wipe away any excess oil from the outside of the insert, and never allow any oil to spill on the gourd surface.

VARIATION

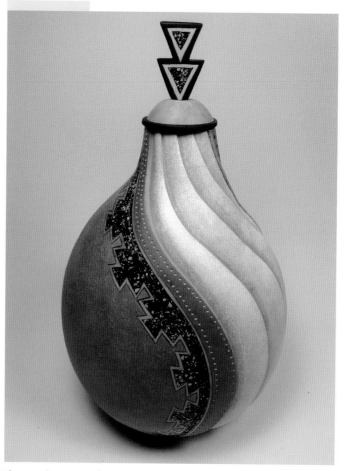

This ripple project features a lid and inlaid stone.

TURTLE BOX

This painted gourd has a charming surprise: the turtle is actually a lid. Bring an attractive stem into play as a decorative handle, or add a small figure riding on the turtle's back to give this southwestern-style container even greater appeal.

Materials

- medium bushel basket, canteen, or round gourd, cleaned
- acrylic paint
- gold leaf (optional)
- heishi beads or seed beads (optional)
- flat black spray paint
- clear spray sealer (matte or semigloss)

Optional Materials for Figure on Lid

- air-dry clay
- wooden beads, drilled for stringing:
- 1-inch- (25-mm-) diameter round wooden bead
- ¾-inch- (20-mm-) diameter round wooden bead
- six ⁵⁄₁₆-inch- (8-mm-) diameter round wooden beads
- 1-inch- (25-mm-) long oval bead
- small dowel
- wood glue

Tools

- small handsaw or mini-jigsaw with a fine saw blade
- sandpaper
- artist's sea sponge
- paintbrushes
- wood-burning tool
- rotary tool and cutting burs (optional)

SELECTING AND PREPARING THE GOURD

1 Select one of the rounder gourds, a bushel basket, canteen, or cannon-ball, for example; choose one with a flatter bottom that sits well, without tipping. If necessary, smooth the base with a file or belt sander to make it level, or build it up with air-dry clay.

2 Draw the turtle lid on the gourd's top, using the pattern given here, or devise your own decorative lid design. Cut the lid along the line, using the guidelines below.

CUTTING A SHAPED LID

Take the guesswork out of putting the lid in its proper position: design it with a notch or graphic element that indicates clearly where it fits in the opening.

Cut the lid at an angle toward the center of the gourd. This angled cut creates a ledge upon which the lid can sit.

Don't cut in "trapping" elements that lock the lid in place. Notice in the project illustrated here that all the appendages (the turtle's neck, head, legs, and tail) are contoured to end in points or pointed curves, with no recesses cut in. Any such cut-ins or inward-angled cuts (such as cutting the turtle's neck narrower than its head) will lock into the gourd's natural curves, and snap or break off. Formulate a design with all obtuse angles (greater than 90 degrees) for a lid that removes and replaces without a hitch.

Use the thinnest blade available to cut the lid. A saw blade removes material as it cuts; the width of the cut it creates is called the "kerf." Remove the minimum material possible to allow the lid to fit neatly without "sinking" into the base.

Some brands of mini-saw have relatively thick blades that produce wide kerfs. Alleviate this problem by substituting inexpensive coping saw or scroll saw blades. Sold at hardware stores, these blades are usually a standard size of 5 inches (12.5 cm), sometimes with a small pin at each end. Choose blades that have 15 to 18 teeth per inch (TPI) and are the correct width for the slot of your mini-saw. Snip the blades into appropriate lengths with a wire cutter. Be aware that these modified blades are thinner and more fragile; they require a lighter touch with the saw. With patience and practice, you can make very fine cuts with them.

Make a starter slit with a sharp hobby knife at each angle in the turtle lid design. Remove the saw blade from the gourd and insert it into a new slit when you reach a corner.

The Turtle Lid Pattern

A little care and patience in the cutting produces a lid that needs minimal trimming and sanding to finish.

Paint the gourd interior black, and burn into the shell a pattern of reeds swaying above a stream, represented by a pair of wavy lines.

Do not drill a hole to begin the cut; make a slit first with a hobby knife to create an invisible line. Place the tip of the knife blade on the line where you want to start the cut, and rock the blade back and forth until it pierces the gourd shell and makes a small slit. Insert the saw blade into the slit to start cutting. For more intricate designs, make starter slits in several places; don't try to cut around narrow angles. The turtle here, for instance, has sharply pointed toes; make a starter slit at the tip or base of each toe. When you reach another angle, remove the saw blade and insert it into a new slit as you cut around the toes.

Take your time; cut around the design slowly and carefully. Hasty work makes for crooked cuts and broken saw blades, and lid-cutting slips are hard to fix; trimming, cutting, and sanding only widen the gap between the lid and the bowl.

If after the initial cutting, the lid seems to stick or be difficult to lift off, check first that all the cuts at corners and angles are complete. Cut with a hobby knife through any areas that may not have been fully sawed. More often, the fibrous inner lining of the gourd makes the lid stick. Insert the hobby knife blade as deeply as possible into the cut, and wiggle it gently to break these fibers. Repeat this process around the cut line until the lid breaks free.

3 Scrape and clean the underside of the lid and the gourd bowl interior thoroughly to remove the inner pulp and seeds. Be careful not to remove too much material, as it may affect the final fit of the lid. Use the same care when sanding any rough edges on the lid and bowl. The lid's underside usually has a mounded area where the stem grows. Sand this smooth or leave it intact, as you prefer.

Never use water to soften or help remove the pulp and seeds from a lidded gourd. Like wood, gourds swell and even change shape a bit when wet. Wetting will soften and permanently relax the gourd's natural curvature, making the lid no longer fit.

Spray the interior of the gourd with flat black spray paint. Be sure to coat all the cut edges of the lid and bowl with paint; the added thickness will make the lid more snug. Wipe away any paint over spray on the lid or exterior of the gourd with a cloth dampened in solvent.

4 Add decorative designs to both the turtle lid and the bowl, using a wood-burning tool. The example here has a pair of wavy lines, representing water, encircling the bottom third of the bowl. Burn in graceful reeds or water plants here and there above the "stream." Embellish the water's surface with a strand of inlaid beads for greater impact, if you like.

CREATING A FRAMEWORK FOR AIR-DRY CLAY EMBELLISHMENTS

5 If the gourd lid has a nice stem, leave it in place to serve as a handle. Consider adding a sculpted figure to ride atop the turtle.

The figure here is a *Mudhead kachina*, or *Koyemsi*, a clown or comic figure appearing in ceremonies of the Hopi tribe. Its name derives from the mud bulges applied to the figure's mask. Use this or another character for the lid—the same construction techniques apply, whatever character you choose.

For added strength, start with a framework of wooden beads and air-dry clay. Assemble the wooden armature from beads of different sizes and small pieces of dowel; configure them any way you like.

Insert a dowel through the two largest beads to form a torso, and attach them with wood glue. Ensure that the dowel extends a bit from the lower bead. Drill a hole in the center of the turtle lid, and glue the short dowel into the hole.

Glue on the small beads for eyes, ears, and mouth. Finish the back of the head with a round bead, or half of an oval one. For a more secure bond, lightly sand the end of each bead to enlarge the gluing surface. Set aside to dry completely before adding arms and legs.

Construct the limbs from air-dry clay. If the arms will stick straight out from the body, reinforce them with an additional piece of dowel. Drill a hole on each side of the "body" bead, and add a piece of dowel or toothpick; then build the arm over this wooden "skeleton." Arms placed close to the body need no reinforcement. Apply small clumps of air-dry clay, and shape it into arms and legs with your fingers or a tool. Use damp fingers to smooth and refine the clay.

Repair any cracks that develop in drying with a bit of fresh clay. Allow the clay to dry completely before sanding or painting.

The turtle lid features a burned design, and will bear a wooden figure. To the figure's armature will be added arms and legs, fashioned from air-dry (paper) clay.

Sponge paint the "stream" in shades of green or blue, and splatter it for effect.

Small decorative dots carved along the bottom of the stream add a last, extra bit of punch.

PAINTING AND FINISHING

6 Paint the bowl with acrylic paints. Blues and greens are most effective for the wavy stream. For added interest, cover the surrounding areas with a protective masking, and sponge or splatter paint over the base color. Remove stray paint with light sanding, using fine sandpaper.

Sponge the base of the gourd with thin layers of accent color that contrast pleasingly with the water, and highlight the area with a light sponging of some metallic paint.

Decorate the reeds or water plants with a mixture of techniques: painting, burning, carving, or gold leafing.

7 Paint the lid only after the clay is completely dry. Paint the Mudhead deep brown, with black and white bands around his arms and legs, and on his stomach. Lightly stroke a dry brush with a hint of white paint on the features as a decorative accent.

Paint the turtle with the same group of colors used on the gourd bowl. If desired, leave some areas unpainted or add accents in dimensional paint.

8 Spray the completed bowl with a clear sealer. Apply the finish before adding optional embellishments, such as gold leafing or inlay.

Add details to the lid. Dimensional paint gives the appearance of embossing for a wonderful raised effect.

LIDDED BOWL WITH ANTLER HANDLE

*A faux-finished patina and natural materials combine in an elegant
lid that makes a superb contrast to the untouched beauty of this
stunningly simple gourd bowl.*

*Use this recessed lid when you wish to change the profile of the bowl by
adding a rounded top or unusual shape lid. This type of lid sits firmly and
securely on the bowl.*

Materials

- canteen gourd, cleaned
- scrap gourd piece for lid
- metallic patina paints
- patina oxidizers
- matte acrylic sealer
- flat black spray paint
- wax or other finish, as desired
- stick, antler, pinecone, or other material for handle
- short piece of ³⁄₁₆-inch (5-mm) dowel

Tools

- compass
- small handsaw or mini-jigsaw
- burning tool
- rotary tool with sanding drum
- sandpaper
- drill with ³⁄₁₆-inch (5-mm) drill bit
- glue
- old paintbrush

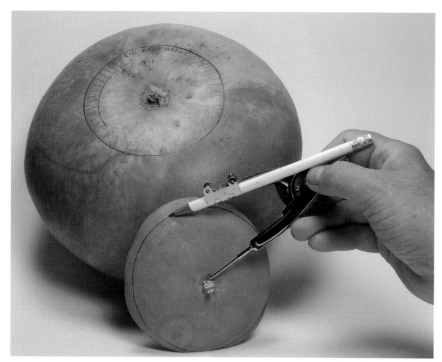

With a compass, draw two concentric circles on the gourd top to indicate the opening and the rim, and one on the gourd scrap that will be the lid.

CREATING A RECESSED LID

1 Choose a gourd scrap for the lid that will complement the bowl's shape. Use a compass to mark two concentric circles on the top of the gourd, centering them on the stem area. Draw the circles so there is a ½-inch (13-mm) wide space between them.

On the large gourd scrap, draw a circle of the same size as the larger (outer) circle.

2 Cut the gourd open along the inner circle, using a mini-jigsaw or handsaw. Clean the gourd interior thoroughly, and spray it with flat black paint.

3 Cut the circle from the marked gourd scrap, and sand the cut edges smooth. Place the circular lid on a sheet of sandpaper, and sand the bottom until the piece lies flat.

4 Use a drum sander to reduce the ½-inch strip on the gourd between the circular opening and the larger circle. Test fit the lid in the opening; the lid should sit evenly on the small lip you created. Sand the lip until it is flat and the lid seats properly.

Carve or sand away material around the opening in the gourd to create a lip where the lid will rest.

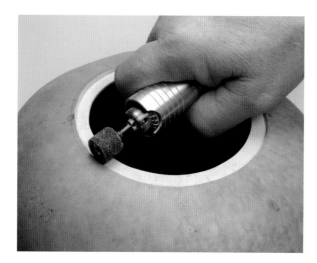

EMBELLISHING THE LID

5 Gather sticks, antler pieces, a sturdy pinecone, or other suitable natural materials, and choose one for the handle. Drill a ³⁄₁₆-inch (5-mm) hole in the center of the lid and the underside of the handle piece, where you want it to attach. Glue a short section of dowel into the handle and test fit it in the lid. Sand the lid or handle for a better fit, if needed; do not glue the handle to the lid until the patina finish is applied.

6 Paint the lid and the lip of the gourd bowl with metallic patina paint. In most cases, it will take several thin coats to achieve good results. Metallic base paints come in a variety of finishes, including copper, steel, iron, and bronze. Each of these produces a different look, and you can use them all with a number of oxidizing solutions for even more diverse results.

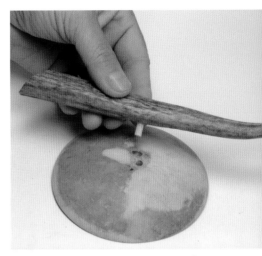

A short dowel reinforces the bond of glue that connects the antler handle to the lid.

Experiment with a variety of sticks, antler pieces, and other natural materials to find a piece you like for the handle.

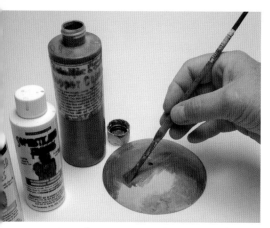

Metallic coatings and a variety of oxidizers create a genuine patina finish.

METALLIC PATINA PAINTS

TIP: Do not confuse metallic patina paint with ordinary metallic craft paint; this special formula actually contains small metallic particles that change color when treated with oxidizers. Many craft, art, and hardware stores stock metallic patina paint and patina solutions.

Apply the patina oxidizing solution while the final coat of paint is still damp. Patina solutions are available in several colors; for this project, I used a mixture of blue and green. Spray, brush on, or splatter the solution, taking care to shield adjacent areas. Don't apply a heavy, uniform coat of solution; an uneven application that allows some of the underlying metal to remain unchanged gives the best results. Every result will differ, owing to minor differences in the application and the nature of oxidation. The patina effect develops as the paint dries and cures. When completely dry, apply a matte acrylic sealer. Finish by gluing the handle into the lid, and set aside.

The patina finish ornaments the lid, and highlights the rim and part of the geometric design.

7 Add visual interest by burning a decorative design around the rim of the bowl. Add small areas of patina when the burning is complete. Use a pattern similar to the one shown here, or create your own. Keep in mind that a simple design and natural finish focuses attention on the unusual lid.

8 Seal the bowl with paste wax or other finish, as desired. Paste wax in a rustic pine adds a degree of color here, and accentuates the gourd's natural wrinkles, marks, and other blemishes. Apply the wax by rubbing with a soft cloth, let dry, and buff to a shine.

FETISH BEAR LIDDED VESSEL

The fetish bear is a common southwestern theme, and is easy to carve and decorate. If carving a simple relief seems challenging at first, you can master the technique easily with just a little practice. A complementary lid made from gourd and wood scraps, a simple inlay, and a fetish bear handle finish the piece with balance and style.

Materials

- round or pear shaped gourd, cleaned
- scrap gourd piece for lid
- acrylic paints
- metallic patina paints
- patina oxidizers
- clear spray sealer (matte)
- flat black spray paint
- scrap pine lumber
- ⅛-inch (3 mm) thick basswood
- ⅛-inch (3 mm) dowel

Optional Materials

- heishi or seed beads, strung
- stone cabochons
- decorative buttons

Tools

- compass
- small handsaw or jigsaw
- burning tool
- rotary tool with burs and sanding drum
- sandpaper
- drill and ⅛-inch (3-mm) drill bit
- hole saw (optional)
- wood glue
- paintbrush

SELECTING AND PREPARING THE GOURD

1 Choose a gourd that sits well and has adequate room for the design. If you are using a round gourd, create a perfectly round opening by drilling with a hole saw. For a pear shape gourd, remove the top by cutting straight across, and retain the scrap piece. Sand the cut edges as needed, making sure the opening remains as round as possible.

2 Clean the gourd interior thoroughly, removing all pulp residue, and spray the interior with matte black paint.

CREATING A STOPPER LID FROM MULTIPLE PIECES

The four components of the lid. The fetish bear handle and lid stopper are cut from scrap pine; the lid base is cut from basswood.

3 The lid has four parts: the stopper, base, dome, and handle. Mark an appropriately sized circular stopper on a piece of pine scrap, using a compass. Cut the stopper with a jigsaw or scroll saw. Use a small belt sander, file, or sandpaper to sand and smooth the edges of the stopper until it fits the opening. Make the fit just a bit loose: later layers of paint or finish will add a little thickness, and can make the stopper bind. Round the stopper's bottom edge with sandpaper.

Cut the lid base from piece of basswood. Sold in many craft and hobby stores, basswood comes in a range of thicknesses. Cut the lid base larger in diameter than the opening in the gourd shell; it should extend about ¼ inch (6 mm) outside the opening. Smooth and round all edges of the lid base; then center and attach the wooden stopper to the bottom. Attach the parts with a thin layer of wood glue, clamping them while the glue sets.

The piece cut earlier from the top of the gourd makes the lid dome, or use another suitable scrap. A functional lid needn't use this extra piece, but it gives the finished vessel a nice contour and greater integrity. If desired, leave the stem as a handle, or use a fetish bear. Complete any carving on the lid dome before gluing it to the base or handle. Glue the lid dome to the top of the base, making sure to center it.

Cut the fetish bear handle from scrap pine. If using the bear pattern shown, size it in proportion to the gourd you've chosen. Cut the bear with a jigsaw or scroll saw, and drill or cut the round opening between the legs. Round over and smooth all edges of the bear with files or a sanding drum, and sand the completed handle.

To make a solid connection between the bear handle and the lid, first drill two small holes in the bottom of the handle, and corresponding holes in the lid dome. Cut and glue two short pieces of dowel into the holes in the handle. Paint or decorate the handle before gluing it into the lid dome.

LOW-RELIEF CARVING

4 For my vessel, I spaced three bear images evenly around the gourd. Use only one, if you like, or add even more, if your gourd is large. Make a prominent display of the bear when you lay out the pattern on the gourd; add decorative bands above and below to complete the design.

> **TIP:** Expressly for clarity in the photos, the patterns here were drawn in bold black marker. Draw the bear patterns with a pencil to make adjustments easy. Remove extraneous marks with a baby wipe or damp cloth.

Decorative half-circles around the bears focus the viewer's attention and provide "windows" for carving; the curved line at the base complements the wavy accent band just below. The bears will be raised in relief by carving away some of the gourd surface around them, in this case, from the window area.

CARVING TEXTURED BACKGROUNDS

5 Remove the dense gourd shell before texturing; carve it away with a rotary tool and structured tooth carbide burs, high-speed steel cutters, or sanding drums. For sharp, clean margins around the window openings, use a wheel, inverted cone, or cylindrical bur to remove the material; cut with a ball or round bur in the center, where you want no sharp edges. Always take care to avoid carving too deeply, and piercing the shell.

Cut the fetish bear handle from a scrap piece of pine; round and smooth the edges with files or a sanding drum. Two dowels secure the handle to the lid.

The vessel and lid are assembled and ready for decorating.

Draw the design on the gourd surface, creating three symmetrical sections.

Fetish Bear Patterns

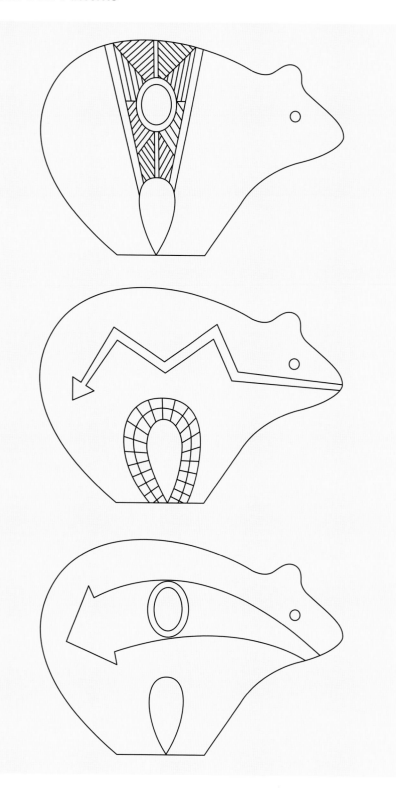

Texture the window background by stippling with a ball-shaped cutter. After removing the hard exterior shell, it's easy to carve the soft inner "meat." Add tiny pits or depressions evenly all over the surface, using a rotary tool and a small ball cutter. Run a piece of medium sandpaper across the carved area occasionally, to mark any high spots and make it easier to see where more texturing is needed.

Carve away the gourd skin from around the fetish bear pattern, using a rotary tool and structured tooth carbide burs, high-speed steel cutters, or sanding drums.

Use a ball bur to incise decorative stippling in the background.

6 Carve decorative bands with a small wheel bur or burn them with a burning tool (see detailed instructions in Ripples and Streams, page 121). Apply seed or heishi beads by inlaying them into channels cut along one or more of the decorative bands.

You may inlay small cabochons or other decorative accents by cutting channels in the desired areas. Do not glue any of these materials into their channels until after all painting is finished, and the final finish is applied and dry.

Make the initial cut for the bead inlay channel with a narrow-diameter wheel bur.

7 Lightly mist the base of the gourd with a spray stain, both to darken the gourd and disguise the area where the base was sanded flat. Carve the tiny accent dots with a ball bur after the stain is completely dry.

This particular gourd has minimal decorative painting; its basic coloration is that of the natural gourd shell. Some decorative bands had a treatment of metallic patina paints and oxidizers, while black acrylic coats the borders and the bear handle.

Enlarge the channel to the proper size with a ball bur.

8 Spray the completed gourd with a clear sealer; matte sealer gives a nice finish to carved surfaces.

9 As a final step, glue beads, stones, or other inlay materials into the precut channels.

The three sides of the finished vessel.

INLAID JEWELS

Dimensional "jewels" (brightly colored, iridescent pieces of dichroic fused glass) give this gourd distinctive dazzle, and you can do the same with gemstone cabochons, buttons, or cameos. Burn in simple geometric designs to frame the inlaid pieces and top the gourd with a scrap wood lid featuring a graceful, classic handle.

Materials

- canteen or other suitable shape gourd, cleaned
- flat black spray paint
- 3 matching dichroic glass or stone cabochons
- oil paint or other coloring agent
- turpentine or blending medium
- wood and gourd scraps
- chopstick rest or other decorative handle
- adhesive (epoxy or gap-filling cyanoacrylate glue)
- clear spray finish (matte)

Tools

- small keyhole handsaw or mini-jigsaw
- drill and a 1½ or 2 inch (38 or 50 mm) hole saw
- hand file or sandpaper
- compass
- small paintbrush
- burning tool
- rotary tool with ball- and wheel-shape burs

CLEANING AND PREPARING THE GOURD

1 If necessary, level the bottom of the gourd by sanding or filing, so it sits evenly. Mark one or more level lines around the top portion of the gourd, and use the lines to help identify the best place for the opening. You'll use these lines later to position the inlaid stones (see Inlaying Cabochon Jewels, page 142).

Cut a perfectly round opening at the top of the gourd, using a drill and a hole saw.

TIP: You can make this gourd without a lid, or cut a simple lid directly from the gourd.

2 Clean the gourd interior thoroughly. Smooth any rough edges with a hand file or sandpaper, and spray the interior with flat black spray paint.

TIP: Cabochon (*cab*, for short) is a jeweler's term for a rounded stone with no facets, and a highly polished surface.

CREATING A LID

3 Construct a lid from wood and gourd scraps, as outlined in Lidded Bowl with Antler Handle, page 132, or Fetish Bear Lidded Vessel, page 136. For the best fit, make the lid only slightly larger than the opening, and cut it from a domed section of gourd that complements the shape of the bowl. Use a compass to draw neat circles for the lid and the stopper. The small size of the opening makes the best choice a simple lid, using only dome and stopper sections. No lid base is necessary. Glue the stopper directly to the dome's underside.

Trace around the handle piece where it will rest in the lid. Cut around the margins of the area with a wheel bur, and inside the area with a ball bur.

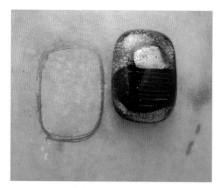

Trace around the stone or glass piece where you plan to glue it on the gourd. Hold it in place with double-stick tape or adhesive putty, if necessary.

Carefully cut inside the traced outline with a ball-shape bur. Remove material, testing frequently, until the stone fits neatly into the recess. Owing to the curvature of the gourd shell, the recess will be deepest at the center.

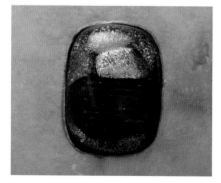

The stone fits snugly in the opening.

Make the handle an unusual object, such as a chopstick rest, wooden carving, or drawer knob, or fashion your own from scrap wood or other material. Finish it with paint or stains.

Because the gourd lid is rounded and the chopstick rest is flat, you must inlay the handle in the dome. Place the handle piece atop the lid dome where you want to affix it, and trace around the piece to mark the area. Cut the outside edges of the marked area with a wheel bur, and remove material from inside the cut lines with a ball-shape bur. Test fit the pieces, and adjust until the handle fits neatly. Complete all other lid decoration before you glue the handle in place.

INLAYING CABOCHON JEWELS

4 Use the pencil guidelines drawn in the first step above to position the cabochons. Place the pieces at the same level and at equidistant points around the gourd. Mark the back of each piece with a number to indicate its placement, and an arrow, its orientation.

Use double-stick tape, adhesive putty, or your fingers to hold the stone in place while you trace around it. Pencil the corresponding number from the cabochon just above the outline. Repeat this step with each stone.

5 Carefully carve away the area inside each penciled outline, using a rotary tool and a ball-shape cutter. Cut slightly inside the outline on the first pass; a hole too small is easily enlarged, but one too large is tough to shrink.

Carve the inlay area deep, flat, and level enough so the piece fits securely in it. Because the inlay recess is cut into the gourd shell's natural curve, the center will be deeper than the edges. A ball-shape bur gives the opening a rounded margin, ideal for fused glass inlays. Stone cabochons, which often have much sharper edges, may call for additional trimming in some areas. Trim with a hobby knife or small bur, as needed.

As you complete each opening, mark the appropriate reference number in the carved area to keep it visible through the rest of the steps. Finish all the decorating and painting before gluing the cabochons in place.

DECORATING AND FINISHING

6 Plan and draw designs to be burned into the gourd. Add a straight band around the gourd's circumference, or a wavy or zigzag line. Draw a frame around each stone, filling and decorating the area with a series of lines

or geometric shapes. Burn the marked lines carefully, and use very fine sandpaper to remove any burnt residue. Wipe dust from the burned lines with a tack rag or an old toothbrush.

7 Apply thinned oil paint of any color to the gourd's base to impart a transparent leather-like finish. Thinned oil color is transparent enough reveal the natural gourd markings, and has superior non-fading qualities. Choose a color that complements the inlaid stones or glass. Substitute leather dyes, inks, or paint, for a slightly different appearance.

Thin the oil paint with turpentine or a blending medium until the mixture is easy to spread with a finger or cloth. Rub the paint onto the gourd surface, and use a small brush to get into tight areas. Add one or more colors until you like the results.

Oil paints dry very slowly; you'll have to set the gourd aside for several days before the next step. You can speed up the drying somewhat by placing the gourd briefly in a warm oven, but do this with caution. Use the lowest setting possible to avoid damaging the gourd.

8 Finish the piece with a light spray of paint or stain around the opening. Add some carved dot accents around the border, using a rotary tool with a ball-shape bur; add a few matching dots or accents to the lid.

9 Spray the completed gourd and lid with a clear finish.

10 Last of all, glue the glass or stone pieces in place. Match each stone to its proper recess, and glue in place, using either two-part epoxy or gap-filling cyanoacrylate glue.

VARIATION

Burn in a design that frames the inlaid glass. The stones bear marks that match them easily to their respective places on the gourd.

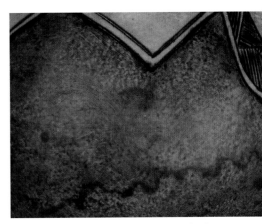

The base of the gourd has a coat of oil paint. A thin layer adds color and allows the gourd markings to show through, and oil paints resist fading.

An alternative gourd piece featuring inlaid jewels.

FAUX BASKETRY VESSEL

Transform a covered vessel into a bold, dramatic work of art with inlaid bands of stone and carved faux basketry panels. It may appear complicated, but creating faux basketry is actually a simple progression of basic carving. With just a little practice, the realistic appearance of your faux coil basketry will have even the most experienced basket weavers shaking their heads.

Materials

- canteen or similar gourd, cleaned
- flat black spray paint
- four matching stone cabochons
- leather dye (brown, honey, or tan)
- wood scraps for lid construction
- scrap gourd piece for lid
- resin or chip inlay kit (turquoise)
- synthetic turquoise nuggets
- short piece of ¼-inch (6-mm) dowel
- adhesive (wood glue, gap-filling cyanoacrylate glue, or two-part epoxy)
- acrylic paint (dark brown, black)
- spray wood stain
- clear spray lacquer (semigloss)

Tools

- small handsaw or mini-jigsaw
- mini right-angle disc sander or other sanding tool
- drill and ¼-inch (6-mm) drill bit
- 1¾ or 2 inch (4 or 5 cm) hole saw
- hand file
- sandpaper
- compass, pencil
- rotary tool
- burs and accessories (ball, inverted cone, wheel, drum sander)
- small paintbrush
- burning tool

CUTTING AND PREPARING THE GOURD

1 If necessary, file or sand the gourd's base to make it sit flat. Draw a series of level lines around the upper portion of the gourd to help identify and mark the top center. Do not erase or wipe them off; you'll use the lines later to place your designs and the panels for carvings and inlays. Cut a perfectly round opening at the top center of the gourd, using a drill and hole saw.

2 Clean the gourd interior thoroughly. Smooth any rough edges with a hand file or sandpaper. Spray the interior with flat black spray paint.

CREATING A LID

3 Construct a basic lid, using wood and gourd scraps, as in Fetish Bear Lidded Vessel, page 136. The small size of the opening calls for a lid with only a stopper and a lid dome. Cut the lid dome from a top or other domed section of scrap gourd, selecting a piece that complements the gourd shape overall. Use a compass to mark a neat circle on the scrap, making the lid about an inch (2.5 cm) larger than the opening.

Make the stopper from a scrap piece of wood. Draw a circle the same diameter as the opening, using a compass. Test fit the cut piece, and sand or file as needed to attain a proper fit. Glue the stopper directly to the underside of the lid dome. Fill any small gaps with wood filler. When the filler has cured, sand and smooth the area, and ensure that the lid still fits.

Make the handle from scrap wood or other suitable material, in any shape you like. Feel free to experiment until you find one that suits both you and the vessel. Cut and sand the handle.

Attach the handle to the lid, using a doweled joint. Drill ¼-inch (6-mm) holes in the base of the handle and the top center of the lid. Insert a short piece of ¼-inch (6-mm) dowel into the handle, and fix it with wood glue. After all the carving is complete, glue the handle into the lid.

The gourd bears marks for the design, and parts for the lid (stopper, dome, and handle) are cut and prepared.

Carving and stippling the adjacent background surface raises the turtles in relief. Carving neatly and precisely is easier if the design's outline is burned first.

LAYING OUT YOUR DESIGN

4 Position the designs, using the pencil lines drawn around the circumference in step 1. Add a series of vertical lines dividing the gourd evenly into eight sections.

Between each set of vertical lines, draw a symmetrical arch; make the arches peak midway between the lines and reach their lowest points right at the vertical lines. The arches should peak at a horizontal line drawn about 2 inches (5 cm) below the gourd's cut opening, and the lowest points should be at a similar horizontal line a third of the way up the gourd's base. Draw a second set of arches at an even interval above the first to create an arched border.

Add a horizontal band that appears to be behind the arched border, no more than halfway down the gourd. The band will create arched "windows" under the arched border.

Create a circular border around the top of the gourd, including an area for chip inlay. Burn the border designs into the gourd, using a burning tool. You can later burn in other decorative lines or borders.

5 Draw a small turtle in every other arched window, and fill the remaining four with a basketry design. Mark each of the basketry windows with evenly spaced horizontal lines about ⅜ to ½ inch (10 to 12 mm) apart. These lines must be level and even to create the illusion of inset basketry panels.

6 Carve the background area around the turtle design; burn the design outline first to make carving easier. Use a rotary tool with a ball-shape bur to remove the material between the turtle and the arched border. Add decorative stipples (closely spaced dots carved into the surface) to the background area.

7 The center of each turtle's back will feature an inlaid turquoise cabochon; select stones sized appropriately for the turtle shells. Use a rotary tool and a small ball bur to carve the inlay recesses (see Inlaid Jewels, page 142, for complete instructions). Test fit each cabochon, and mark the recess and the back of the corresponding cabochon for easy matchup later.

If you like, embellish the turtle shell surrounding the recess, using a burning tool.

CARVING FAUX BASKETRY

8 Carve faux basketry in the remaining four arched window panels. First, use a rotary tool and a wheel bur to cut all the marked horizontal basketry lines and the outline of the window.

Next, use an inverted cone-shape bur to recess the interior edge of each panel slightly. Place the edge of the bur into the groove created by the wheel bur, and follow this line completely around the inside of the arched window area, slightly lowering the edge.

With the same inverted cone bur, lower both sides of each horizontal basketry line. When this is finished, the panel will have the appearance of mounded rows or coils.

Smooth and even the carved rows, using small riffler files, sandpaper, a drum sander, or other tools. Remove all the gourd skin to expose the inner surface on each row.

Accentuate the basketry effect by adding a series of burned lines simulating basket fibers. Burn the first series vertically across each row, spaced slightly unevenly to look natural. Add another series of shorter, lighter lines at the top and bottom of each row.

Carry the carved basketry effect onto the lid surface. Draw a set of concentric circles around the lid, and carve the basket coils in the same manner.

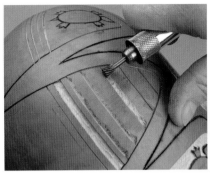

The initial step in carving faux basketry is to cut the lines with a wheel bur. Follow up with an inverted cone bur to reduce the edges adjacent to each cut line.

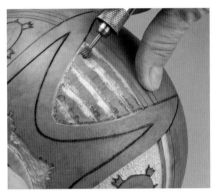

Both sides of the cut lines have been lowered, producing rows of mounded coils.

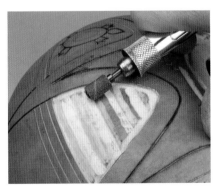

A drum sander smoothes each coil, and removes any remaining dark gourd skin.

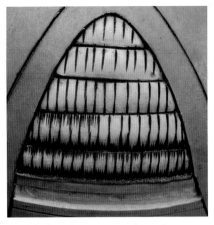

Add further dimension to the coils, using a burning tool. See the progression of the burning from the top row to the bottom.

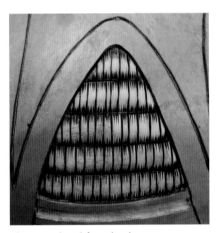

The completed faux basketry carving and burning. A bit of thinned paint provides the final accent.

Recess the areas to be inlaid with resin. Use wheel and ball burs to remove the material.

Resin inlay has been placed in the prepared channels. The resin is mounded slightly to allow for shrinkage in the curing process.

A small disc sander quickly grinds away most of the excess resin. Do the final sanding by hand.

INLAYING WITH RESIN

9 The vessel here has three sections of chip or resin inlay: one circling the top of the gourd; a small band around the middle; and triangular sections in the lid handle.

Use a rotary tool and burs to carve the recessed areas for resin and chip inlay. A wheel-shape bur cuts neat, straight edges; use ball burs of various sizes to remove the rest of the material.

The recesses don't have to be deep: ⅛ inch (3 mm) is usually sufficient. Undercutting the edges slightly will lock the cured resin firmly in place. Be sure to keep the top edges of the recessed areas neat and clean, because these edges will show on the finished piece. Use a hobby knife with a sharp blade to trim edges and remove extraneous material.

SAFETY TIP: All resin products have a strong odor; use them only in a well-ventilated area. I highly recommend you wear a vapor-rated respirator, especially if you are sensitive to strong fumes. If the uncured resin comes in contact with your skin, immediately clean the area with rubbing alcohol or acetone, and wash thoroughly with soap and water.

10 Add the resin inlay material to the gourd only after all carving and burning is complete. Mix the resin and catalyst in specific proportions, according to the manufacturer's instructions. Be sure to use only paper cups for mixing; the resin may react with some plastic containers.

Do not mix big batches of resin; a very little of the mixture fills a large area. Most resins begin to cure and harden within 10 to 15 minutes, so prepare only the amount you can use in that time. Warmer air temperatures will speed the rate of cure and reduce the working time. Do not add extra catalyst to speed the curing; excess catalyst will actually hinder the curing process.

Plain resins containing only dye are thinner than stone and resin mixtures, and may tend to flow out of the recessed areas. Use a thickening agent with these, or create "dams" of clay or masking tape around the channels to keep the material in place while it cures. Work on small sections on only one side of the gourd when using thinner mixtures.

Use a wooden craft stick or disposable spoon to place the resin mixture in the recessed areas. A toothpick is useful for working the mixture into edges and corners. Overfill the recessed area slightly to allow for the resin's settling and shrinking. Let the resin bulge a bit above the gourd surface.

Fill all the recessed areas with the resin mixture, and set the gourd aside in a warm place until the resin has completely cured. Curing will continue even after the material becomes firm; allow at least 8 hours before grinding down the excess resin.

> **TIP:** Some people place masking tape over the design area and cut the recess through the tape; others apply masking fluids around the cut edges of the recess before adding the resin mixture. The masking tape or fluid acts as a protective coating during the sanding operation. When grinding reduces the resin to the level of the masking material, it's time to switch to hand sanding.

Grind the resin material smooth and flush with the gourd surface as soon as it has cured completely. A small disc sander is the perfect tool for grinding resin, and it works quickly. If one is not available, use a rotary tool with a drum sander. Begin with medium grit sandpaper, and grind the cured resin until it is nearly flush with the gourd surface. Then, switch to fine sandpaper, to avoid marring the adjacent gourd shell. Finish smoothing the surface with hand sanding and very fine sandpaper. It takes a delicate touch and a bit of practice to sand the resin without marking the neighboring surface; at first, you may have to add a painted border around the inlay to cover small flaws.

Occasionally, small air bubbles or voids may cause pits or holes in the surface of the resin. If these are large or unsightly, repair them with a tiny bit of added resin. Let the added material cure, and repeat the smoothing process.

Buff or polish the resin surface to a high sheen with a buffing wheel and polishing compounds, or apply a coat of clear gloss for an easy and attractive finish.

A dyed "burled" finish adds color and burned accents decorate some of the borders. The faux basketry pattern carries onto the lid and paint highlights some of the coils.

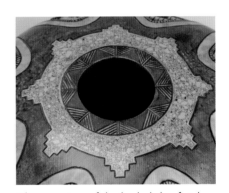

Close-up view of the burled dye finish, with resin inlay and decorative border.

FINISHING THE VESSEL

11 Create a faux burled-wood finish on the star-shaped top of the gourd, using a paintbrush and leather dye. Apply an even coat of brown, honey, or tan leather dye, taking care to apply the dye only in the desired areas. While the initial coat of dye is still slightly damp, touch the tip of the wet paintbrush to the surface. Make a series of dots, spacing them fairly

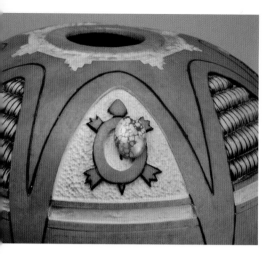

As a final step, glue turquoise cabochons into the recesses carved into the turtles' backs.

evenly around the dyed area. The application of the dye dots will slightly lift the first coat of dye, causing it to bleed and spread in interesting patterns. Repeat this dotting process until you achieve the desired look. Allow the treated surface to dry thoroughly before applying any additional finishes.

12 As an option, darken the base of the gourd with a light mist of spray wood stain to disguise sanded or flattened areas. Use a light touch on the spray to blend the color upward on the sides of the gourd, giving an almost airbrushed effect.

13 Add any other decoration before applying the final finish. You might use a rotary tool and a ball-shape tip to add some carved accent dots around the borders, or a burning tool to burn decorative lines or additional borders.

Complete the basketry areas with a minimal application of thinned paint. Thin dark-brown acrylic paint to a watery consistency, and apply a little bit to the most deeply recessed areas of the basketry carving. The paint will produce shadowing, adding depth and dimension to the finished basket. Accent the basket rows with black acrylic paint.

Finish the lid by highlighting the basketry carving with paint, burning a border around the inlaid resin on the handle, and painting the handle with black acrylic paint.

Spray the gourd with several light coatings of semigloss lacquer. Buff the final coat of lacquer to a soft sheen, using fine steel wool. This rubbed finish produces a smooth satin-like feel.

14 The final step is to glue the turquoise cabochons in place. Match the stones to the openings, and glue them in place, using two-part epoxy or gap-filling cyanoacrylate glue.

Emerging Visions—
A Gallery

Several different artists, each with a fresh perspective, have contributed gourds to this gallery. All use a combination of effects, including wood-burning, intricate cutting, inlaying, carving, and unusual painting techniques or materials. Over time, most artists develop a signature style that makes their work recognizable and distinctive. If you are willing to invest time trying out new ideas and techniques, your own style will surely emerge.

Kachina Shards.

Jigsaw Puzzle Gourd

Ponderosa Forest Dweller.

Mayan Jungle.

*Artful carving and painting give
the vessel a distinctive look.*

Wild Horses, *Phyllis Sickles.*
*Deep carving and burning add
depth and realism to this design.*

Various untitled figures, Julie Jurow.
Photo by Julie Jurow.

Stylized Kachina figures are painted with acrylics, and embellished with leather, horsehair, feathers, wood, and tin.

Untitled, Rob Ghio.

Rob Ghio uses an innovative embellishment: he carves on emu shell and inlays pieces into the gourd.

Big Foil Fish, *Carla Bratt.* Photo by Cody Bratt.

This gourd was treated with a mixture of paints and metallic foils.

Sausalito, *Rebecca Shelly.* Photo by Rebecca Shelly.

This fascinating gourd teapot features acrylic paints, found metal objects, clay, beads, and a metal bowl.

Sticks 'n' Stones, *Cindy Lee.* Photo by John Stacy.

This gourd has been treated with resin inlay and burning, and has a trim of woven sticks around the top.

Desert Jewel, *Dave Sisk*. Photo by Dave Sisk.

Mask making at its finest. Dave Sisk decorated this gourd shell with dyes, colored wax paste, and carving, and embellished it with horsehair, sinew, African porcupine quills, brass cones, beads, and a variety of feathers.

Pomo Basket.

Rows of coiled basketry on this vessel are embellished with glass, feathers, and beads of bone and shell.

Ancient Overseers.

ACKNOWLEDGMENTS

A truism holds that artists stand on the shoulders of all of those artists who came before them. Just so, a good many people have influenced my work over the years, from my distant grandmother, a basket maker and a full-blooded Delaware Indian, to the gourd artisans of every description who so freely lent their expertise. Special thanks go to a number of people who provided technical assistance, and kindly shared their knowledge.

Leah Comerford, who produces beautiful, intricately rendered illustrations on gourd surfaces, was most generous in sharing her expertise in the use of watercolors on gourds.

Darienne McAuley graciously shared instructions on techniques for coil weaving on gourds. Her unselfish spreading of her knowledge has inspired many budding weavers. Unknowingly, she taught me an activity I could do on long car trips—and this has saved my husband hours of backseat driving. He thanks Darienne, too.

Phyllis Sickles is not only a great friend, but one of the most inspiring gourd artists I have had the pleasure of knowing. Our endless hours of experimenting, carving, and creating have been invaluable, and she has motivated me to set ever-higher goals.

Cheryl Dargus was a fantastic "guinea pig" and proof-reader, spending hours checking the projects for readability, and the directions for ease of understanding.

Jim Widess patiently talked me through all the initial stages of writing this book, and offered me invaluable advice along the way.

Above all, my thanks and gratitude go to my patient husband, Everett Gibson, who has encouraged me, supported me, and tolerated the mess for so many years.

INDEX

ABOUT THE AUTHOR

Bonnie Gibson has delved into a wide variety of three-dimensional art forms over her 30-year artistic career. Completely self-taught, she has won awards and recognition for her work in scale miniatures, woodcarving, scrimshaw, and other sculptural media.

"I discovered gourds quite by accident. While attending a local craft fair, I picked up what appeared to be a large piece of Native American pottery. It was amazing and exciting to discover that the item was actually made from a gourd, and I could hardly wait to try working with them!"

Bonnie combines a wide variety of skills and techniques with her deep appreciation of the native cultures of the Southwest in creating unique gourd vessels and sculptures. Well known in the gourd community for her distinctive style, she is represented by several fine art galleries, and her artwork has won acclaim, including multiple Best of Show awards at competitions and exhibitions. She is highly sought after as an instructor, and her articles on gourd art have been published in *The Gourd*, *Through the Gourdvine*, and *Gourd Art Today* magazines. Books that have featured her work include *The Complete Book of Gourd Carving* by Jim Widess and Ginger Summit (Sterling, 2004) and *Beyond the Basics: Gourd Art* by David MacFarlane (Sterling/Chapelle, 2005).

Her Web site, Arizona Gourd Creations (www.arizonagourds.com), is very popular for the tutorials, activities, and creative inspiration it offers.

Bonnie holds a Bachelor of Science degree from Bemidji State University in Minnesota and a Master of Science from the University of Arizona. She enjoyed a brief career as an athletic trainer before retiring to rear her two children. Those years as a stay-at-home mom allowed her to explore and enjoy art as both a hobby and a business.

Bonnie is a long-time resident of Tucson, Arizona, where she lives with her husband, Everett, and several pets, including a cat and a cockatoo.

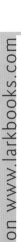